Brave Enough

Embrace Your Fears, Cope With Your Anxieties

and Build Self-Confidence –

Use Obstacles To Your Benefit

By Zoe McKey

Communication Coach and Social

Development Trainer

zoemckey@gmail.com

www.zoemckey.com

Copyright © 2018 by Zoe McKey. All rights reserved.

Illustrations by Mixed Media Artist, Karen Dawn

No part of this publication may be reproduced, stored in a retrieval system, or transmitted in any form or by any means, electronic, mechanical, photocopying, recording, scanning or otherwise, except as permitted under Section 107 or 108 of the 1976 United States Copyright Act, without the prior written permission of the author.

Limit of Liability/ Disclaimer of Warranty: The author makes no representations or warranties with respect to the accuracy or completeness of the contents of this work and specifically disclaims all warranties, including without limitation warranties of fitness for a particular purpose. No warranty may be created or extended by sales or promotional materials. The advice and recipes contained herein may not be suitable for everyone. This work is sold with the understanding that the author is not engaged in rendering medical, legal or other professional advice or services. If professional assistance is required, the services of a competent professional person should be sought. The author shall not be liable for damages arising herefrom. The fact that an individual, organization or website is referred to in this work as a citation and/or potential source of further information does not mean that the author endorses the information the individual, organization or website may provide or recommendations they/it may make. Further, readers should be aware that Internet websites listed in this work might have changed or disappeared between when this work was written and when it is read.

For general information on the products and services or to obtain technical support, please contact the author.

Thank you for choosing my book! I would like to show my appreciation for the trust you gave me by giving **FREE GIFTS** for you!

For more information visit www.zoemckey.com

The checklist talks about *5 key elements of building self-confidence* and contains extra actionable worksheets with practice exercises for deeper learning.

Learn how to:

- Solve 80% of you self-esteem issues with one simple change
- Keep your confidence permanent without falling back to self-doubt
- Not fall into the trap of promising words
- Overcome anxiety
- Be confident among other people

The cheat sheet teaches you three key daily routine techniques to become more productive, have less stress in your life, and be more well-balanced. It also has a step-by-step sample sheet that you can fill in with your daily routines.

Discover how to:
- Overcome procrastination following 8 simple steps
- Become more organized
- Design your yearly, monthly, weekly and daily tasks in the most productive way.
- 3 easy tricks to level up your mornings

Table Of Contents

Introduction 13
Chapter 1: On Courage and Bravery 23
Chapter 2: On Confidence 47
Chapter 3: Which is my way? 55
Chapter 4: Every Time You Win 67
Chapter 5: Fear of Loss 77
Chapter 6: Fear of Failure 97
Chapter 7: Do One Thing Every Day That Scares You 107
Chapter 8: Don't Miss Your Shots 127
Chapter 9: Start By Doing What's Necessary 149
Chapter 10: Unlearning Versus Learning . 161
Chapter 11: Curiosity Will Conquer 175
Chapter 12: Life After Success 185
Chapter 13: Courage To Accept Mediocrity 203
Final Words 217
Endnotes 225

Introduction

Imagine the following two scenarios.

Scenario one. The meeting ended later than expected. It is cold and dark outside. A storm is gathering in the distance and you can already see winds and lightning. You shiver, tighten your jacket's collar, and start walking home. It is silent and your footsteps are echoing as you walk. Your mind starts spinning wildly about why there are so few people on the street. You know that this area is not particularly safe. Your father used to say that if someone is out on the street on a night like this, they are probably up to no good. You quicken your pace when a shadow suddenly moves into your peripheral view. Despite your best instincts, you freeze and you can feel sweat drip down your face.

Scenario two. Your husband just found some incriminating pictures on your computer of another man. Right now he is questioning you about it. You know what you did was wrong, and there is no right answer to fix this situation. The questions are so paralyzing mentally that you can't even follow what you say. You just talk. You lie. The pictures belong to your friend. You just saved them. You know that it sounds incredibly stupid but you were so unprepared to have this conversation that your brain just ran away, leaving you in this mess. Your husband becomes angrier and you're even more lost. Your stomach is squeezed to the size of a peanut, and your heart beats so violently you fear it will stop at any moment. You feel dizzy and nauseous.

These two scenarios are fairly different but they have something in common. *Fear*. It is a safe bet that you have felt both of these kinds of fears at least once in your life. The difference between them is that the first scenario is mostly self-triggered fear based on imagined danger, while the second is legitimate fear based on real events. We experience both kinds of fear on a daily basis; not stepping in front of a speeding car is driven by legitimate fear, while fearing that someone deliberately will drive on the pedestrian walk just to kill you is imagined fear.

We encounter so many fears in our lives: fear of heights, wide spaces, narrow spaces, spiders, snakes, water, fire, flying, and

15

going underground. These types of fear are hardcoded in our genes. For millions of years, these fears were legitimate, and our very survival depended on our hyperactive sense of fear. They knew if they fell off a high cliff, they die. If they get bitten by a spider or snake, they die. These factors directly threatened human survival.

Humans developed other type of fears, too: fear of loss, being alone, dying, conflict, and rejection. These fears, while they don't seem to pose an imminent danger to survival, could indirectly lead to it. If someone lost family members, was alone, got into a conflict, was rejected or expelled from a community, their survival chances dropped significantly from being alone.

Today, fear is depicted as something bad in most self-help literature. It's seen as something one should get rid of, defeat, or try to escape from. However, fear is not less natural or necessary as other emotions like love. Fear is an essential response to physical and emotional danger.

Without fear we couldn't protect ourselves from real threats. But times have changed. On one hand, most of the threats that were legitimate before are no longer. On the other hand, there are instances where imagined fears cause us to miss opportunities that are right in front of us.

There are some fears that we learn during our lifetime. These are usually connected to a trauma or bad experiences. Whenever we experience anything resembling our past traumas, our brain can trigger a fear response within us that is hard to tranquilize.

How does fear work biologically? Fear is created by our brain. It is a chain reaction which begins with a stressor and concludes with the release of chemicals. These chemicals are responsible for a racing heart, energized muscles, and faster breathing. We call this the fight-or-flight response.

The stressor can be anything from a stick that looks like a snake, hearing a gunshot, imagining your audience before a speech, or the shadows of tree branches blowing in the wind.

The brain is composed of more than 100 billion nerve cells. These create a complex network of communications that is the ground zero of everything we think, feel, and do. There are communications that lead to conscious thoughts, and there are communications that create autonomic responses. Fear as a response is almost always autonomic. It is not our conscious decision to become fearful, and by the time we acknowledge consciously what's going on, fear has invaded us. Our brain cells are working without stopping; sending and receiving information, there are many parts of the brain that are involved in generating fear as a response. The main parts of the brain involved in this process are:

- The thalamus: this determines where to send incoming sensory data (from the ears, eyes, nose, mouth, and skin).

- The sensory cortex: this is where we interpret sensory data.

- The hippocampus: this stores and recovers conscious memories. It processes the incoming stimuli to diagnose context.

- The amygdala: this decodes emotions, determines if we are in danger or not and stores fear memories.

- The hypothalamus: this activates the "fight or flight" response.[i]

These all happen within milliseconds.

Fear is a natural emotion that can't and shouldn't be erased. Without having sensible trepidations, we'd end up in the hospital more frequently than we are. There are, however, some things that trigger a fearful response even though they shouldn't. We learn to be afraid of certain things in our life that are not life threatening or scary at all. More so, they are causing us to live an unfulfilled life. This book aims to help you overcome the irrational and harmful beliefs that make you fearful, and allow you to experience life from a perspective of courage and fearlessness.

You'll read about the following:

- · How to make the first step when you debate starting something new.
- How to be more confident.

- How to make the best decision when you meet a crossroad in life.
- How to keep your ego in check.
- How to handle the fear of loss.
- How to thrive in failure.
- How to let go of your fear of missing out.
- The importance of doing something every day that scares you.
- How to stop judging people and let go of judgment.
- How to have the courage to learn something new and let go of the old.

And much more.

Chapter 1: On Courage and Bravery

"Behold the turtle. He makes progress only when he sticks his neck out."

-- James Bryant Conant

Illustrations by Mixed Media Artist, Karen Dawn

For free classes on how to take your learning to a deeper level using creative sketch noting and art journal techniques please www.thevisualjournal.com

The turtle, like most animals, is an instinctual being. It peeks out of its shell to go somewhere because it is hungry or to look for a calmer and better environment. Its actions are not conscious. If the turtle could think and analyze its station in the food chain hierarchy, it would probably never come out of its shell, and it would die of hunger.

Just like turtles, a person risks his own wellbeing, reputation, or safety when he sticks his neck out. He risks being misunderstood, ridiculed, contradicted, attacked, shamed, threatened, or ignored... A person who sticks his neck out does something even though he knows he may not succeed. He could fail. Still, there is a drive stronger than the fear in this act.

It doesn't matter what drives you. Maybe you have a burning passion to do something; or maybe you are a more calculated, cold-headed person; or even someone with less obvious ways of achieving self-fulfillment. Something drives you. There is that hidden or well-phrased idea, wish, or dream you haven't chased yet inside you. All of us have wishes beyond the basic human instinct. All of us wish for something more, something deeper, something that makes that special difference we cannot always articulate. Usually we refer to this as a "purpose."

Be brave and courageously daring to unleash your purpose from the realm of your mind and into the land of your actions. Go through the wall of your fears, knowing that there are some bumps in the road in every journey.

Why did I mention bravery and courage separately? Because they have different meanings. The words may seem similar, but the actions involved in their practice are different. They also have the potential to turn into pride, hubris, and cause more damage than good.

Conventionally, they are considered synonyms. According to thesaurus.com, they both mean boldness, fearlessness, and a state of mind that gets you through obstacles, difficulties, and challenges. These are all true. But they also pump your blood differently. Let me explain the difference between bravery and courage with two examples.

Bravery is the ability that manifests itself in the absence of fear. Brave people confront danger, pain, and situations considered to be impossible without much critical judgment. It is strength of character that, in most cases, is learned from family or society and becomes a habit, second nature.

Brave people usually seem bigger than the challenge they are facing. They may seem majestic, even heroic. Often, they are the main character in an action movie or a tale.

A good example can be found in the movie, *300*. For those of you who haven't seen it, the movie is about Leonidas I, the warrior king of the Greek city-state Sparta, who decides to go against the will of other Spartan leaders and confronts the enormous army of the Persian king, Xerxes, with only a small army of 300 Spartan warriors. I don't want to spoil the movie for you, so I'll just share the major theme of the film. These 300 men weren't afraid of their odds against a vastly larger enemy. They confront the Persian Army, despite its massive size. Based on the battle they willingly sought out, the movie's title could have been Mission Impossible just as easily as 300. They challenged the odds, so we consider them brave. Their glorious bravery is the highlight of the movie.

Brave people are those one-in-a-million heroes who seem to never fear, question, or hesitate before jumping into a battle, or out of an airplane with only a parachute. They cam eat worms or stepping onto the stage without the slightest jitter of nerves. These people just blow your mind one way or another.

But what's with the rest of us, the other millions of people who aren't that brave? Who didn't grow up in a family or environment that taught the mastery of fear? What about those of us who never get, or seek the chance to prove ourselves as mighty heroes? What can we do? What ability can we rely on to get what we want? How do we learn to be brave when we've never been taught how?

Courage is the answer to these questions.

Courage, in contrast to bravery, is a mindful act, fueled by emotion. Courageous people feel the presence of fear, but still undertake that overpoweringly painful, difficult action. Courage is more than an ability. It is a state of mind led by the conviction that the reward makes the risk and effort worthwhile. Unlike brave people, courageous people feel less capable of succeeding in the face of the challenge. Courage is not so much about winning as it is about making the choice to fight, even if it may have severe consequences.

One great example of courage is in a cartoon that ran in the 1990s called *Courage the Cowardly Dog*. The protagonist is a little dog that is exquisitely fearful. He freaks out when he sees his own shadow. Still, when monsters, ghosts, and other scary creatures attack his master, Courage never hesitates to protect her. He faces his fear out of love for his master. In this case, the main message of the show is not the fact that the dog is courageous, but in his motivation, why he does it. He does it out of love.

Other similar heroes include Sam from *The Lord of the Rings* and Neville Longbottom from the Harry Potter series. They are not the main characters, but their roles are necessary for the protagonist to win.

Courageous heroes usually don't do impressive things. They are those who overcome their own limiting beliefs, fears, and demons. They take action despite their fears.

Find your reasons for being courageous. What do you love? Who do you love? What are the things and people for whom you could be a hero? What if you discovered that you are the very person you should be the hero for?

Say yes out of self-love or say yes out of love for others if you feel, on a gut level, that's the right thing to do. Get over your trembling knees, your wildly beating heart, or all those groundless fears you convinced yourself were real.

Just take a deep breath, take the first step, and stick your neck out.

Don't get me wrong. I'm not encouraging you to jump in front of a bullet or volunteer in the Hunger Games. Most courageous acts are not loud or visible. It takes courage to apologize if you do something wrong to others. It takes courage to take responsibility to your actions. It takes courage to open up your heart and love someone else – or yourself – with all its might. It takes courage to forgive, to let go, and to fully live.

I read this on Quora one day and liked it so much that I saved it to my personal quote collection. The author of the thought, Bodhisatwa Paul Choudhury, is an Indian gentleman who grasps courage very well.

"The first step takes courage. The first step inside a cold pool takes guts. There are voices asking you not to take the dip, not to go ahead, to maintain the status quo, to let it be. Only when the first step is taken, you realize that it's not all that bad! You are now confident. You want to take another step, see what lies beyond. Fear gives way to curiosity, and forging ahead seems easier.

But the first step is not the hardest. The hardest step is the one that you take when you are tired and have walked long enough, and yet there is

> no oasis in sight. You know it will not be one glorious first step now, but an infinite number of steps, which might not lead anywhere. Worry not about the first step. There are harder times ahead..."

We are educated to consider the first step to be the hardest. We have dreams to chase but the words, "the first step is the hardest" echo in our minds. The word *hard* is instantly associated with pain, risk, and fear. This is why most dreams die before they've even begun. And with them, we die a little bit ourselves. Our time is running out whether we enjoy our ride on this earth or not – that day, month, or year will pass regardless of our choices.

The hard part is staying courageous on the road. Have you ever done a 2000 meter row challenge? Or a 2000 meter running challenge? I have. The first 500 meters always seem easy. I am still fresh, I'm in the zone, and I pay attention to the time. The same goes for the last 500 meters. The middle kilometer is the deal breaker. That requires the stamina and mental strength to stay present. That determines the outcome of my time, not the first steps and not the last steps.

This rule applies to almost everything in life. Practicing courage, sticking your neck out to achieve something, is no different.

"Courage is the ladder on which all other virtues mount."
 --Clare Boothe Luce

Did you know the word courage originates from Latin? Core means heart. Being courageous means following your heart.

Courageous people are not undefeatable. They are, in fact, quite vulnerable, but that's what makes them great.

You need courage to start living your life. Be who you are, love someone with your whole heart and, have the courage to make mistakes sometimes. Embrace your vulnerability; it makes you beautiful.

Courage is the ladder that will help you reach all the wonders that may now seem impossible to obtain. If you feel intuitively that you want to do something else, that something's missing from your life, take the leap.

> *"Have the courage to follow your heart and intuition. They somehow know what you truly want to become."* – Steve Jobs

I wrote my first book at the age of twelve. It was a story about six kids who found themselves in an extraordinary situation and needed to grow up earlier than expected. I spent all my free time writing that book. After finishing it, I showed it to my literature teacher who, after taking a glance at, it didn't encourage me to continue my writing career – if you know what I mean. I listened to her and didn't write a word of literature for more than ten years. As a kid I had given up easily, but I'd always felt something was missing. The thoughts and stories in my head screamed to be put on paper, but I resisted that calling.

It is natural to fear taking action, especially if you've been criticized in the past. But look inside yourself. Is fear of failure your only motivation? There is more to this life than trying to escape our fears.

If you, for example, work someplace you hate, don't settle for it. Plan to change it. Not immediately, you'll have to pay your bills somehow, but slowly set your mind and heart to change. Maybe you are a car mechanic because your dad was a car mechanic. He taught you what he knew with the best intentions and gave you all the skills he had so you could survive, just like him. Be thankful for that. But if you'd really love to be a chef instead, take steps toward that goal. After all, you already know how to handle oil...

Start small. First watch some YouTube videos and try to recreate the meals. Then apply for a free course for aspiring chefs. Then take an inexpensive class. Become engaged. Keep track of your improvement. Maybe it will take months or years. So what?

One of my first readers, and now dear friend, Joe M., stuck his neck out in a very inspiring way. He read my book, *Find What Your Were Born For* about two years ago. He sent me a thank you email – one of the firsts I ever got – on how much my book had helped him. He realized that he had been treading water for about twenty something years at a company where he worked very hard, but still was not appreciated. He expected to get a promotion for his uniquely hard work ethic and loyalty, but decades and decades later this remained an expectation. Joe was at a dark place when we first talked. He felt discouraged, unfulfilled, and sad.

He told me that my book felt like a little light at the end of the tunnel for him. After reading it, he opened his eyes more to opportunities. He consciously sought them. One day I got a message from him that he had left his old job and would soon start working at a totally new company. He was happy, excited, full of positive expectations, and most importantly, he was relieved of a huge amount of stress caused by his previous job. Luckily, his amazing family fully supported him in his adventure.

Almost a year has passed since Joe changed workplaces. I decided to interview him and use his words as a reference for all of you pondering making the same move as Joe.

1. What was your main motivation to leave your old place?

"Knowing that there has to be something better and refusing to allow fear to prevent me from better job opportunities."

2. Why were you afraid to make this step before?

"My greatest fear was the unknown and worrying about future states that have not even happened. I allowed the fear to drive me to change."

3. How is your life better now?

"My life is better now because of feeling appreciated and knowing I can come to my job with enthusiasm and a team that's supportive and not destructive to my self esteem. Sometimes the best thing an employer can do is to pat you on the back and tell you, "good job." No pay raise can give you the great feeling that this simple deed can accomplish."

4. What are your current challenges (if any) at your job?

"My current challenge now with my new job is learning as much as I can to be a more valued employee that will continue to be appreciated as part of the team. I LOVE my job! This is something I have not been able to say in over 28 years! I am truly liberated and free from a horrible past employment! Lastly, it was your books that helped me gain the confidence to make that leap! I'm still soaring too! Thanks from the bottom of my heart Little Zoe!"

I must say, if my books never helped another person, the experience was already worth it. I was so greatly, deeply happy for him and incredibly proud that he had the guts to make this leap after spending time at a workplace for... well almost for as long as I have inhabited this planet.

Of course, Joe's path isn't challenge free. He has to adapt and learn a great amount of new skills. He might have been an unhappy veteran at his old workplace, but here he is "the new guy" and has to prove himself to his team and supervisors.

Brian Tracy, a motivational speaker and life coach, says that it takes eight years of reading and researching a topic for one hour per day to become an expert. Most people generally say eight years is too long of an investment. His reply, yes, maybe, but those years will pass anyway, regardless if you start reading or not.

Being courageous and embracing who you really are isn't easy. Most of the time it is difficult and challenging, and you need to go through a dip before you start rising again. But if you stay true to yourself and work diligently

– not for anyone else's pleasure or to satisfy your ego – your hard work will pay off.

Exercises for this chapter:

1. Today I did this courageous act:

   ....
   ....
   ......

2. Today I took this first step:

   ....
   ....
   ......

3. Today I have taken this next courageous step in something I've already started:

Chapter 2: On Confidence

"Each time we face our fear, we gain strength, courage, and confidence in the doing."

- Theodore Roosevelt

Confidence is a tricky topic, one we only tackle when we feel we don't have much. This being said, how can we gain confidence when we have no experience in being confident? For example, how can we act confidently in our new position when we've never worked in that domain before? How can we be confident our newest relationship will work out for the better when we have never had a healthy, balanced relationship before? How do we ask out someone on a date when we have never asked anyone out before (or haven't for a long time)?

If you believe that you lack confidence, it may seem to you that those who you perceive as confident are getting more and more confident as time passes while you, and the people who lack confidence, just dig themselves deeper and deeper into a hole with each failure. Sure enough, if you've never felt accepted by your peers, you'll act meekly and unconfidently around them. They will perceive you as someone who lacks confidence and is awkward. This will be even more rejection. You'll sense this unease and consequently have even less confidence to socialize. It is a vicious circle.

If I've stepped on your heart now, because this is exactly how your life is, don't get discouraged. How could you reasonably expect yourself to feel like a confident winner if you've only experienced losses? Winners act like winners because they know the feeling. If you've experienced mostly losses, guess how will you act… It's not about you. You are not a loser if you've come to that conclusion. Your circumstances caused your way of acting. The only problem is that in order to become more confident, you need to win a few times and adapt to that state of mind. But to be able to win, you need to act confidently. Here it is, your catch 22.

Now you may wonder with a loss of hope how you can you breakout of this devil's loop?

It is not easy, but it's possible.

First, you need to redefine confidence. Just like when we say, "how do you become successful," what we really mean is, "how do you become rich," when we say confidence, we mentally link this state to some external factor. If someone is generally accepted as rich, beautiful, or smart, we automatically assume he or she is confident. However, we could fill books with the name of wealthy people who lack confidence in their money, stars who question their beauty, and professors who lack confidence in their own knowledge.

It is safe to assume that the real confidence we are aspiring for can't be defined by some earthly standards. It is something intangible, something that roots in our mind, the perception of ourselves. Based on this affirmation, it is not hard to see that if we only improve the external aspects of our lives, it won't necessarily make us confident..

You can lose twenty pounds, get your beach body, and still lack confidence. You can get straight As and still feel like you're a loser. You can make your first million and have poor self-esteem. Marrying someone, or having a kid won't build more confidence in an ill-working relationship.

Confidence can't be described by tangible things or events. It is rather a state of mind. It is a conviction (much stronger than a belief) that you are enough and you have all you need to do well in life. For example, someone who is poor and has mediocre education, but is confident in his social skills, will get on much better in society than someone who is rich and educated, but is also spastic, and socially awkward. In theory, the second person has everything in his sleeve to be accepted in society, but his *perceptions* of himself don't allow it. He perceives that he lacks something essential to be accepted. And this assumption will drive him to act strangely in a social setting. In other words, it is not him who messes things up, but his assumptions in lacking something.

No. The key to confidence is not simply the belief that one lacks nothing in the world. This kind of thinking leads to a false self-image. If you've never made a profit in your life from your business, it is dangerous to believe that you lack no business skills. Or if your BMI is over the roof, it is unhealthy to think that you have the perfect weight. It won't do you any good. You'll just act as an oblivious person with narcissistic affiliations.

The key to confidence is being aware of what you might lack AND being comfortable with it. Our confidence does not show up when we achieve something, but when we don't achieve something and we are still capable of loving ourselves and not internalizing the failure as a personal weakness. Confident people are good conversationalists because they are comfortable with small talk too. Confident business people are confident because they can stomach losses.

Confidence is not the celebration of success, but the acceptance of the negative. At some point in our lives we all realize that personal growth comes from painful lessons; the most rewarding business decisions root in substantial losses.

In our awesomeness-seeking culture, failure is so ostracized that we believe that if we become comfortable with it, we will become a failure. This is a lie; don't believe it. When we become comfortable with failing, quite the opposite will happen: We will be able to be courageous, to initiate great conversations, and engage in unknown situations because we realize we have nothing to lose. If we end up failing, the sun will still set in the west and rise in the east; and when it does, we will try again. Because we know that if we persist, we'll win. This is true confidence.

Exercises for this chapter:

1. Today I let go of this external metric of measuring my confidence:

....

....

2. Today I felt comfortable with this failure:

....

....

Chapter 3: Which is my way?

"When two paths open before you, take the harder one."

--Nepalese proverb

Illustrations by Mixed Media Artist, Karen Dawn For free classes on how to take your learning to a deeper level using creative sketch noting and art journal techniques please www.thevisualjournal.com

All of us arrive to some crossroads in our lives from time to time. Usually one of the paths we can go on is harder and the other is easier. Needless to say, that the harder path seems scarier or riskier so many end up walking the same old, safe road. This can be a wise decision in some cases: drive on safes roads and buy food from trustworthy sources, etc. But when it comes to choices of self-development, the harder path hides the most growth potential almost all of the time.

When evaluating the harder path we have three options:

Say yes

Saying yes takes courage; it takes guts. If you feel in your gut that the harder path can make you a better person (and you want to become a better person), take it. Do not worry about how you will face the challenges on the path when you make the decision. Jack Canfield said, *"Our job is not to figure out the 'how.' The 'how' will show up out of the commitment and belief in the 'what'."* Chose the harder path when you are absolutely committed to it, when you know it is the right thing to do.

Wait and delay the decision

When you are not 100 percent sure about what you want to do, it is wiser to wait, look at all your options carefully, and explore your thoughts and feelings about each path. Ask yourself:

- What do you want?
- What do you need?
- What can you do right now?

Do not delay the decision for more than a week. One week is usually enough to do your research in almost any field. If one week is not enough to make a decision, double check why are you still hesitant? Make sure you are not just procrastinating on the issue. If you do procrastinate, analyze why:

- Are you not really that interested in making a decision about X?
- Are you afraid in making a decision about X?
- You know you don't want X, but outside factors put pressure on you to go for X?

You know, there's the roadside knowledge saying that if you hesitate about something for too long, it means your answer is probably a no.

Some people procrastinate because they want to do four, five, or six major things in their lives and they don't know which one to choose. Nor do they want to rush into a decision.

Relax. If you want to start five different businesses in your life, you can. The average life expectancy in the United States is seventy-seven years for men and almost eighty-two years for women. Let's be optimistic and assume this best-case scenario. If you are thirty years old, you still have ten years for each business. If you're older, then you'll have proportionally less time, but you can still achieve at least two or three main goals.

Don't be like the donkey that cannot decide whether to drink or eat first so it dies of hunger and thirst in the midst of indecision. If you have more hard paths and you cannot choose, then be courageous and rely on the answer to the third question: "What can I do right now?" Be brave and choose the hardest of the hard ones.

Say no

This answer is good in only one case: if you are absolutely sure the hard path is not right for you at all. Don't choose no out of laziness or comfort. For example, I could have been an accountant at a good firm. It was a hard path, but I said no because I would have hated to work as an accountant. With all due respect to readers who are accountants, I admire people who are good with numbers and can do this work from day-to-day, but I'm bad with numbers, and I don't like sitting in one place for long periods.

In other cases, saying no can be the result of fear and a lack of confidence. Let me tell you something demoralizing. Walking the hard road is not that special. You're not the first, nor the last trying to make a difficult choice. You're not the first to say no either. There are nameless masses who have said no before you. But consider some of the most famous figures in history: Socrates, Alexander the Great, Galileo Galilei, Joan of Arc, Winston Churchill, George Washington, Abraham Lincoln, John F. Kennedy, Marie Curie, Mother Theresa, Martin Luther King Jr., Buddha, Jesus, Muhammad. These are men and women who said yes to extremely difficult paths in life.

Great things are born only when you are courageously daring. You might not win on the first attempt, but if you persist, you will become more courageous and closer to success.

However, life is not composed of only deal-breaking decisions. In fact, life is a mass of small decisions, and how you react to big challenges depends on how you react to the small everyday life choices.

Let me share the computer scientist and essayist, Paul Graham's small trick with you. It's a way you can motivate yourself to choose the harder way in small life choices; Always present yourself with two options. For example, if you're trying to decide whether to go out jogging or sit home and watch Netflix, go jogging. The reason this trick works well is because people are a creature of comparison. One solitary option means nothing. If you give yourself the sole option of staying inn and watching Netflix, that's what you'll do. There is nothing better or worse in your mind than watching TV. When you have two paths and one is harder, you know that the only reason you're even considering the easier option is due to laziness. When you have two options, one harder (and healthier) you know what's the right thing to do. This trick simply compels you to acknowledge it.

Mr. Graham thinks of it as a trick, but it's much more than that. Choosing the harder path is a lifestyle that requires the discipline of a Spartan, but it's also a way of living a progressive life.

The easy path leads to undemanding mediocrity. But the avoidance of mediocrity shouldn't be your motivation to choose the harder path. Being mediocre is a label, which is stated upon a comparison – in most cases a comparison to somebody else. If you make a choice with the sole purpose of not being considered mediocre, that choice is not about you or for you. You should take the harder way in an effort to grow as a person, spiritually, in strength, materially, or to build something worthwhile that will outlast you. Do this for yourself, not for others.

Exercises for this chapter:

1. Today I chose this harder path:

....

....

2. Today I said "no" to this easier way:

....

....

Chapter 4: Every Time You Win…

"Every time you win it diminishes fear a little bit. You never really cancel the fear of losing; you keep challenging it."
   --Arthur Ashe

Being courageous and experiencing victory makes us bold, which is good to a point. I really love the quote above, but it made me think, and I realized that as liberating as a new sense of victory can be, it can turn us to the "dark side" if we're not careful. What is the "dark side?" How can we avoid it? That is what this chapter is about.

Were you really successful for a period of your life? Did you plan things that worked out well? Even what didn't work out as planned turned to your advantage? You knew there was luck involved, but you slowly attributed your success to your own performance? As days passed you developed a sense of entitlement and pride. Did you walk down the street with headphones in your ears, imagining you were on the Hollywood Walk of Fame and that every person you walked past noticed you being glorious and almighty?

Many of us have experienced something similar at least once in our lives -- after an A+ test, a promotion, getting a book published, or winning a game. Confidence and bravery can be easily built with a series of successes. Victory, positive feedback, and results fill our hearts with satisfaction. There's nothing wrong with it unless it turns into conceit.

Premature pride can be very harmful on the long run. You stop focusing on growth and learning. You cease improving. Premature pride can turn any success into bitter failure. This is why quick, overnight success can be dangerous. In seventy percent of cases, lottery winners are poor again within a few years. They can't handle their money, and they ignore their health.

So what leads to this harmful state people fall prey to? It has many names: over-confidence, arrogance, but maybe the shortest and most descriptive word is ego.

Ego is pure self-centrism. *Me, me, me, I, myself, me...* This is the only thing an egotistical person can see, hear, feel, and acknowledge when they fall too deeply into the rabbit hole of over-confidence. Ryan Holiday defines ego in his book, *Ego is the*

Enemy, as "an unhealthy belief in our own importance. Arrogance. (…) To be better than, more than, recognized for, far passed any reasonable utility - that's ego."

The main problem with ego is that it distorts reality. It gives people the false impression of being more, knowing more, and being capable of more than they actually can. This notion, sooner or later, leads them to failure. Failure is something the ego is not prepared for, nor can it interpret it to be true. The ego's reaction is to make excuses and get angry: *it was not my fault; I'm so much better than that; this is untrue, a very stupid construction of…; not me, it wasn't me*. And so on.

Rage and anger push the egotistical person off a cliff in two ways. One way happens when rage and anger don't cease; they keep pushing the person to repeat the same mistakes without correcting his errors until he fails again and again, becoming depressed but more determined. You know Einstein's classic saying about insanity being a person who does the same thing over and over again expecting different results. Egotistical people become insane in this sense because they become totally cut off from reality.

The second way rage and anger can lead to the total withdrawal from any challenge is when the ego convinces its master that trying the thing she's failed in is totally unimportant. She is very good, so she doesn't have to prove anything to anybody. She knows and that's enough. Whatever the reasons for her failure, they were not her fault; the competition was corrupted, the judges biased etc. Excessive theories about her potential take over her actions, and she becomes the heroine of big words and small actions. You've probably met that guy or girl who knows the game better; who cooks more delicious food; who has more knowledge of something, but if you challenge them to a debate they back off, because they don't have to prove anything to anyone.

Both manifestations of the ego are harmful to your personal development, social connections, and financial career development.

How can one manage the ego?

Forget about appearances; forget about others. In most cases ego arises because people know what you've accomplished. You may also be guilty of working hard for the sole purpose of impressing people. But remember, impressing people and being impressive are two different things.

Practice humility. It is a good exercise to resist the temptation of telling everyone, including your friends, when you've accomplished something. This is really hard because when something extraordinary happens, your first instinct is to share it with someone. Let your friends and acquaintances hear about your success first from someone else. Also, be prepared to be okay with nobody knowing about your success.

Resist the urge to indulge your ego after you are praised, too, otherwise the whole exercise loses its effect. Say thank you for the kind words and continue working hard for your own sake.

Keep your goals to yourself. Not only because sharing them will prematurely boost your ego and lead you to the bad attitudes described above, but also because it is more likely you'll never reach your goal if you share it before completion. Why? Derek Sivers, in his [TED talk](), said that psychology tests have proven that the good feeling spreading in you when you tell your plans to someone will make you less likely to complete them.

To reach a goal you have to complete a series of steps that lead to that goal, right? Normally you'd feel good only after the completion of these steps. You'd feel that you'd gotten closer to your goal, but since you've shared the goal with someone and they acknowledge it, your mind will play a trick on you. Your mental state will be what psychologists call social reality. Because of the acknowledgement, you'll feel the satisfaction of achieving your goal as if it were already completed. Since you've felt this satisfaction, you won't be as motivated to work hard anymore. The ego will be satisfied by the social acknowledgement and attention so it will go back to the nest where he feels entitled to do nothing.

Mr. Sivers advises at the end of his TED talk that if you need to tell somebody about your goal, phrase it in a way that it doesn't cause satisfaction. For example, I really want to win this presentation contest so I have to repeat my speech three times every day until it's memorized flawlessly.

Let's recall the quote at the beginning of this chapter, *"Every time you win it diminishes fear a little bit. You never really cancel the fear of losing; you keep challenging it."* Be courageous. Engage. Put yourself out there. Win. Become more confident. Build bravery and challenge your fears, but do not let your ego ruin your hard work and achievements.

Do not forget, if you win, you win for yourself. To improve.

"Your potential, the absolute best you are capable of – that's the metric to measure yourself against. Your standards are. Winning is not enough. People can get lucky and win. People can be assholes and win. But not everyone is the best possible version of themselves." Ryan Holiday

Learn, strive, and focus on being the best possible version of yourself – for your sake.

Exercises for this chapter:

1. Today I kept quiet about this achievement:

   ....

   ....

2. Today I won against my ego by:

   ....

   ....

Chapter 5: Fear of Loss

"The only person you should ever fear losing in a relationship is you yourself."

— Miya Yamanouchi

Illustrations by Mixed Media Artist, Karen Dawn
For free classes on how to take your learning to a deeper level using creative sketch noting and art journal techniques please www.thevisualjournal.com

If you have lived a few decades on this planet, you're familiar with loss. Losing someone or something leaves a traumatic memory, thus we will naturally be fearful of loss. Depending on what we lose, this emotional state can be one of the worst human experiences.

Certainly, one of the most painful experience is when someone dear to us dies. That is an irreversible, unchangeable fact that we need to get used to. I think that there is no time or magical book in the world that can fully fill the void death creates. In this chapter I won't attempt to do this impossible task. I lost my grandparents (who raised me) more than ten years ago. Yet I still dream with them. I still cry occasionally and miss them dearly. But it's also true that the pain is less sharp today than it was ten years ago.

There are other faces of the pain generated by loss: we can lose a partner, a business, a friendship, an object, or even time and memories.

Now, after dating my partner for more than three years, I can state that it is our habit to revisit the spot in Budapest where we shared our first kiss. Every year we make our little pilgrimage to Margaret Island and sit under the pine tree where we had our passionate, emotion-filled, butterflies-in-the-stomach, totally spontaneous kiss. Who would have thought back then that the, at what felt like at the time, impossible love would last for so long? Hopefully for a lifetime. It was that kind of kiss that you dream of all your teenage years, and if you are lucky, you'll experience it a few times in your life.

While remembering this kiss fills my heart with warmth, I also feel sadness. I was a bit jealous of my past self, that I have experienced that kiss. Now, standing at the same spot with the same person, kissing doesn't feel the same. I don't mean it doesn't feel great, just it doesn't have that curiosity-filled expectation only first kisses born from passionate love can have. We are not the same people we were then. We will never be so madly in love as we were at the beginning of our relationship, and I will never get to feel that excitement again. That's inarguably gone. Despite losing all this for the best possible reason, I still feel touched by the power of the previous experience when we walk off, holding hands in the sunshine.

As you can see, it is not only people and things we can lose. We can lose experiences, beliefs, ideas, and hopes. Everything we lose is a little death. Everything that is gone forever requires us to have a strong coping mechanism, otherwise we fall into the depths of despair. Never is a very tough word and feeling. Never means something is out of our control for good; we can't change it despite our best efforts. This is a scary pill to swallow.

You can't bring someone back to life. You can't turn back time and redo a relationship. You can't get back wasted time. These are gone; and so is a little part of you.

Why does loss feel so bad? Because to feel good in our own shoes, we need to fill our days with meaningful actions and people. When we lose something or someone important, we lose some of our life-fueling meaning. Romantic, family, work, and general human relationships give us the most meaning in our lives. Consequently, losing any of them is devastating. It will leave that proverbial void in us. Depending on the depth of the relationship, the meaning we attach to it can be identity shaping. For example, after a while, we don't only look at ourselves as individuals but also as " the girlfriend or wife of X" or "the accountant of Y company" or "the daughter of Z."

When we lose any of these, a little part of our identity is lost with them. This is what we really mean when we say, a part of me will forever stay with him or that a little part of my identity, of my sense of self, is gone. The more meaningful someone or something is in our lives, the more their loss will shake and change us, because the greater part of our identity will be lost with it.

This is why it is crucial to not depend on and not extract meaning from only one or two of the relationships in your life. Because if you lose one, you might fall into an existential crisis. My grandmother was first and foremost a wife and mother. She was married to my grandfather for more than fifty-five years when he died. They had worked together, lived together, and laughed and cried together since my grandma was nineteen. Soon after my grandpa died, my grandmother also died, without any previously warning or illness. Her reality simply ceased to exist without my grandfather in it. While my grandparents' case is a bit extreme, an almost *The Notebook* style, depression is not an uncommon cause of excessive loss.

Depressed people with strong suicidal inclination, while are inarguably sad, are not depressed because they are sad. They are depressed because they find no meaning in life, say the experts. The deeper in depression someone falls, the less likely he or she will be motivated to do everyday things like get up every day, eat, work, go out… "What's the purpose?" They may ask. "All that is just so meaningless."

Thus, the first step after losing someone or something is to slowly but surely establish new relationships and new activities to bring new meaning into our lives. The worst thing you can do is to dig a hole in the past and deliberately stay there. Refusing to accept that one part of you is gone will lead to a sorrowful life where you won't be able to love yourself without the missing that part. The lack of self-love will make you unable to truly love others. Or ironically, if we talk about a non-death-related loss, your lack of self-love and respect led to your loss in the first place.

How do you recover from a loss? I will answer this question for the most classic loss people seek coping strategies for: break ups.

How do you overcome a break up?

I bet you have already experienced that when you've started a romantic relationship, the world ceased to exist to you. You literally communicated with your friends less often, you called your momma only twice a week instead of daily, and generally all the rest of your human relationships began to atrophy. If you havn't experienced this, I'm sure that you've had a friend who has and, in this case, you were the neglected friend.

And then the bomb dropped. You broke up; and beyond the tears, the what ifs, and broken plates, it sunk in that you were now alone. I by no means want to diminish the pain felt after a break up. It is one of the nastiest, most helpless feelings in the world. On one hand, it feels open ended in the beginning because, unlike death, here the person is still alive and "dum spiro, spero"[1] you

---

[1] While I breathe, I hope. Latin proverb.

can fantasize about rekindling the relationship. On the other hand, deep down, you know that the relationship has ended for a reason that, in most cases, is bad enough to not try to resurrect it.

The best you can do is to let it out of your system. Don't try to pretend everything is okay; don't try to be strong. Just cry it out. Don't do it alone. Surround yourself with the people who truly care about you (your family and those selected friends who still invited you for a beer after the tenth rejection). Their purpose is not only to lend you an ear and shoulder. You need them in your life to establish new meaning. To do this and begin your new life with a clean slate, you shouldn't focus the new meaning around healing the wounds caused by the failed relationship. Yes, you need some time to figure that part out too. But your new objective should be to create a new, happier you, not to patch up the old you. This means finding totally unrelated passions and meaning in your old relationships. For example, don't become more fit just because your ex always nagged you about going to the gym, but you never listened, and now working out makes you feel closer to her and still connected. You'll likely relentlessly post about your new life just to show her that you've changed. Decide to become more fit for your own sake. It is not a bad idea to try to fix the parts of yourself that one way or another led to the end of the relationship. But do it only for yourself.

It can be helpful to overcome break up misery by objectively look back on the relationship. Our memories are deceitful and tend to project the relationship through pink-shaded glasses once it is over, making you believe that you are a terribly bad person who messed up a great relationship that was not so bad at all... I'm here to tell you that relationships never end because of the fault of one singular party. Both parties involved have equal responsibility, even if it's only for one of you being an a-hole and the other for tolerating it.

If you are honest to yourself, you'll discover that the relationship was in fact an unhealthy one to begin with. Many relationships take a toxic turn when the participants interpret drama as caring, jealousy as too much love, and talking in whatever nasty manner as intimacy.

If you can identify your past relationship as an unhealthy one, it is good to take some time off in the relationship business and establish a relationship with yourself. Get to know who you are as a person first. Chances are that your relationship became toxic because you didn't know who you truly are and what you want and neither did your partner. Because if you did know these things, you wouldn't have settle for drama, emotional blackmail, or other destructive behaviors. Don't try to fill the emptiness you feel after the breakup with another person. That's a recipe for disaster.

While you are on your self-discovery journey, you can try and learn from the mistakes of others. Allow yourself to be vulnerable. Talk openly with your most trusted friends or a therapist about the mistakes you think you made. You can get useful advice on how to improve your relationships as well as the comfort of the notion that you are not the first person on the globe who's made the same mistake.

You can also read some books on the topic of dating and failed relationships. My all time favorite book on this subject is *The Five Love Languages* by Gary Chapman.

I could dedicate an entire book for what toxic relationships look like and how to overcome break ups, but I hope I gave you some tips on how to move forward.

How to overcome the pain – and fear – of loss in general?

First, you need to understand that our memories play tricks on us. What is beautifully nostalgic from our teenage years wouldn't satisfy us at all today. For example, when I was in an unhappy relationship, I always told myself that I was unhappy because I wasn't done with my party-flirty time. When I finally became single, I would go to a party, but I felt it to be empty and meaningless. Just because I enjoyed parties at the age of twenty-one, before I became steady with my ex, it didn't mean that I could resume everything where I left it after I became single again. Many things happened while I wasn't it a solid relationship. I graduated and started working seriously. I became financially responsible for my parents, and I grew up. A few months after I broke up with my ex, I met my current boyfriend, and I've never felt regret since. I can't even have empty flirts with random strangers because of the importance of my relationship.

Our minds tend to remember the very good or the very bad. Consequently, something that was rather good seems even better with time, and something that was somewhat bad seems even worse. Our minds seek happiness either in the past or hopes for it in the future. In reality, happiness happens now, here, in this moment.

Second, invest time in yourself. Is there anything you wanted to try, but whoever or whatever you lost prevented you from doing so? Try it now! You always wanted to write a book, but you never had the time? You just got sacked? Write that book! You have nothing to lose. Best case, you'll have a book. Worst case, you'll realize that book writing isn't for you after all. Whatever happens, you'll be richer with information about yourself and experience.

Third, don't try to fill the void your loss left you with the same thing too soon. If you've experienced a breakup, don't rush into a new relationship. Even if your past relationship was not toxic, you still need time to heal and get ready to accept a new person in your heart. If you've lost your job, don't settle permanently in a new job. I know you need to work to pay the bills, but only settle for your new job for long term if you are sure that's what you want to spend your life doing. Otherwise, consider it just for what it is, a bill payer.

Finally, acknowledge that everything is lost eventually, even your life. Think back to your greatest losses. Many of them were necessary to make space for even better, greater meanings. Leaving behind a bad relationship is painful, but without it you wouldn't be able to find the person who you'll live happily (mostly) ever after with. Also, without losing something bad, how could you know that what you have now is good?

Losses, just like pain and failure, are the way to gain perspective and eventually live a better life.

Exercises for this chapter:

1. Today I discovered that losing …….. benefited me with:

....

............…..

2. Today I did these steps to create new meaning in my life:

....

............…..

Chapter 6: Fear of Failure

"Our greatest glory is not in never falling, but in rising every time we fall."

- Confucius

Napoleon Hill once asked the audience at one of his seminars how many times people had decided to pursue a goal before they gave up? The correct answer was less than one. This means that in most cases, people don't even try. They give up before even attempting a shot.

Fear of failure has roots in childhood. When you were little you wanted to discover the world. You had unlimited bravery and approached the road where cars flew by or tried to embrace a beehive like Winnie-the-Pooh. In response, your parents, who were trying to protect you, dramatically made you understand the dangers of such actions. But their reactions often included unnecessary threats that incited fear. Also, parental anger and punishment in a child's mind equals love withdrawal. Every time a person feels they lost love, they will associate the experience with failure, that they had done something new and failed to receive love. As a result, children attach trying out new things with the loss of parental love.

Other children are the victims of overly demanding parents. Every time they brought home a grade worse than an A, the parents were unsatisfied, thus the child felt like a failure.

These children grow up, but at their core they will stay the same. They will fear to try out new things and become perfectionists because they will associate it with the loss of respect and love of their parents. They will fear rejection and humiliation. You will never be good enough for everybody. If an adverse opinion or judgment hits you, evaluate.

Accept that judgment is inevitable, and don't try to fight it. Think it over and if there is some truth in the criticism, do your best to correct it. If you consider the judgment unfair, invalid, and useless, just put it in your "garbage from somebody who doesn't know me" drawer and move on.

I know this is easier said than done, but only you can make this decision. You have to decide whether to give space to the feeling of anxiety and resentment or to control your momentary irritation, consciously analyze it, and remain aware of your values and flaws.

Even the bravest people hit a point where they become insecure about their potential and start to be afraid of success. When doubt hits you, do not stop. Instead, focus only on the next step ahead of you. If that step seems so big that you cannot complete it, cut it into sub-steps. It doesn't matter how many. Let it be the smallest thing, like climbing the stairs instead of using the elevator if your goal is to lose weight.

Just stay in motion. Do small steps diligently, feel the progress, and you'll see that the fear will go away and you'll regain faith. You resisted temptation and didn't stop.

Write a S.W.O.T. analysis for the case you agree to. If you're facing a challenge and numbed by the weight of the decision, take a piece of paper and pretend you said yes to the challenge. Divide the paper into four sections.

Know thyself.

Assessing yourself realistically and being aware of your strengths and weaknesses is an essential tool to overcoming your fear of failure. Why? Because if you are objectively aware of your strengths and weaknesses, you'll make more accurate judgments on what challenges you should engage in. Also, you'll be able to predict some kind of realistic outcome. For example, if you know that you are good at weightlifting, but you are bad at cardio, you probably won't engage in running a marathon. Not with the hope of winning it, at least. However, you could engage in a weightlifting competition with better hopes. If you know your personal records in each exercise you need to perform, that's a great start. But remember, a stand-alone number is not good for much. You need to compare it to other numbers to assess whether your personal record is enough to win the competition. Compare your number with the winning numbers of the last five years. Compare your number with the best weightlifters in the world. This is not to demoralize yourself, but to get an objective picture on where you stand now. This way you can set realistic goals for your weightlifting competition. Imagine if you go there convinced that you'll win and you end up fifth? That would be even more demoralizing than being aware of your current chances.

The best way to make a transparent self-assessment is a S.W.O.T. analysis.

First section: Strengths. Put all the qualities, information, practice, connections, and relevant knowledge you have right now in this section.

Second section: Weaknesses. Write down the things you know you need (knowledge, connections, etc.) but don't have or know yet. Define the particular problems and the questions you face that could be an obstacle in reaching your goal.

Third section: Opportunities. List all your current options for resolving the problems faced in section two. Pay attention to how many of them can be solved and how much time and energy would be required to make sure you overcome your weaknesses. Focus on the time/energy/benefit triangle. Make sure that your goal is worth your time and energy.

Fourth section: Threats. List the possible risks, hindrances or qualities, external threats, lack of resources, anything that is an obstacle in achieving your goal.

If you do this analysis before any major challenge, you'll have a more-or-less clearer picture of what result you can expect. Thus you can rationally diminish your fear of failure. You don't have to conduct a S.W.O.T. analysis to make minor decisions like determining if you should visit your in-laws over the weekend.

Know that very few decisions affect your life in the long term. Most of them don't bear importance a day or a week later. Minor things don't matter enough to torture yourself with the fear of failure. For major decisions you can always do a S.W.O.T. analysis.

Exercises for this chapter:

1. Today I made the following major decision:

   ....

   ....

2. It turned out to be a:

   ....

   ....

Chapter 7: Do One Thing Every Day That Scares You

"Do one thing every day that scares you."

--Eleanor Roosevelt

Illustrations by Mixed Media Artist, Karen Dawn For free classes on how to take your learning to a deeper level using creative sketch noting and art journal techniques please www.thevisualjournal.com

There are a few type of events that "help" us learn to be fearful:

Active repetitive events: This type of fear is often connected with childhood trauma. When a person, as a child, was exposed to destructive criticism or even violent actions he learns to fear them quickly and deeply. For example, if someone was often hit when she was late returning home, she becomes notoriously punctual as an adult. If she runs late occasionally, she will feel stressed and fear punishment.

Passive repetitive events: These events teach us how to be professionally fearful without being aware of it. Remarks like, "we have been farmers for ten generations, and if you aren't going to take on the family heritage you'll be a disgrace." These are remarks that cut deeply and can bring you down. And worse, can convince you to become a farmer even though you wish to do something else.

You can become passively fearful if your parents were afraid of something and they talked about it very often. My grandparents were always afraid of diseases. I was raised in an environment where fear of disease was the main decision-maker. Needless to say, I still fight with a slight paranoia and hypochondria as an adult.

Big traumas: If you fall on the top of the fireplace as a kid, you'll learn to fear fire and hot things in general. If you nearly drown at some point in your life, you'll fear even Evian. If you get stuck somewhere, you'll fear tight spaces. Even thinking about fire, water, or tight spaces could trigger a fear, make breathing hard, and give you sweaty palms. You know what I'm talking about. Big traumas certainly can trigger the most aggressive fear in us.

Self-made discouragement; This mistake is mostly generated in adulthood. Taking on challenges one's destined to fail can lead to the false notion of not being good enough. For example, if someone who didn't exercise for half a year signed up for a half-marathon, chances are he'll fail. Unfortunately, in spite of all the obvious facts that predicted the failure, the only conclusion people draw in similar cases is that they'll never try it again. It's not for them. This attitude can spill over into other life areas, discouraging people from trying out new things in general.

People so often dive into impossible situations to have something to complain about, to seek confirmation from others, or to justify their lack of courage. Continuously failing isn't exactly the remedy to fear and becoming more confident.

The four categories listed above show the type of fears we learn during our lifetime. The first three are rooted in childhood, but the fourth is typically developed in adulthood. As time passes, we start to rationalize irrational fears. Let me make a clear distinction between a rational and irrational fear. Fearing falling on a hot stove when you trip next to it is not irrational. It can happen, and if you are very clumsy you can indeed touch the stove. But starting to freak out when you read about a fire incident in China is irrational. You don't need to triple check your stove being turned off.

Fear of taking risks

Risk is directly proportional to failure. The more risky something is, the greater the chance we'll fail. Since people hate failing, they hate taking risks as well.

How many times have we heard a bank commercial say that something is a low risk investment? "With low profit" is often written in the fine print. Other common sentences include:

- It is a risky question to ask in such an early phase of the relationship,
- It is risky to invest your money in this or that,
- It is risky to contradict a PhD professor; he knows it better.

All these examples stand for different manifestations of fear. These types of fear are all connected with the fear of failure.

Fear of the unknown

We are not fortunetellers. Who knows what tomorrow brings? People hesitate to take action today because they fear the risk of tomorrow. I won't invest in these bonds. When we collect a little money, we fear investing it because we fear losing it.

Without a higher risk, there is no high reward. I don't want to encourage anybody to invest money recklessly. Only invest if you trust your advisor or you have extensive knowledge backed by data about the bonds, firm, or whatever you want to invest in. One of the most common risk-fear connections is the fear of assuming *financial risk*.

The greatest investors and businesspeople engage in high-risk businesses and they get out successfully most of the time. But, even when they fail, they don't collapse. They learn a lesson and try a different approach the next time. These people claim that the risk can be reduced dramatically by following three guidelines:

- having financial knowledge,
- knowing accounting,
- and trusting your gut.

As soon as you have theoretical and practical knowledge, your fear will diminish and risk will decrease significantly. The lack of knowledge is risky in every field. This being said, remember the golden truth, don't keep all your eggs in one basket. If you invest all your fortune in one single thing, you won't have a good night sleep afterward. Who could rest assured knowing that because some force majeure event they could end up on the street? Nobody.

But who said investments have to be so dreadful and doomed for failure? Take investing in a 401(k). It is fairly safe. Let me guide you through a quick calculation. If you just graduated, let's say you're twenty-two and about to start your new job. Throw $50 dollars a month in your 401(k) with a fifty percent company match.

You'd need to pay attention to raise your contributions by the same amount as any pay raises. If you successfully do that, you'll have more than $1 million dollars in your 401(k) account by the time you're sixty-five. (Assuming a 3.5% annual raise and 8.5% return on investment.) Hey, cruises, here you come!

This example, while it has a lot of ifs involved, still gloriously presents the power of compound interest. Even if things don't work out according to the best-case scenario, you'll still have some money set aside for your golden years. If the worst-case scenario happens, and you lose everything, you'll still be okay financially. If you make $1000 a month, that's still only about 1/20 of your entire income.

Investing, anyone?

Fear of rejection

Have you ever pretended to agree with your partner when in fact you didn't? Are you often saying things or acting against your values just to please those around you? Do you fear losing the acceptance of others?

if you answered "yes" to these questions, then you fear taking *social risks*. You may live your life based on others' opinions and requirements. You don't want to assume the risk of exposing your own thoughts because you fear others will criticize and reject you.

However, as time passes, you'll be frustrated by all those disagreements you didn't express. Your inner peace will be disturbed because of the constant internal conflict you experience. The feelings of desperation and guilt will mix in your mind. In the long term, this kind of behavior can result in a physical manifestation, a form of a serious illness.

Accept that you can't satisfy everyone. There will always be people who don't like you or who don't agree with you, but there will be others who do. Approach likeminded people.

Fear of losing someone

The symptoms are very similar to the previous example, fear of rejection, but here the person you try to please is your significant other or the people closest to you, your kids, family, closest friends. This is a situation when you don't want to take *emotional risks*.

When two people meet, they try to show their best sides. It is natural to want to be as appealing as possible to someone we feel attracted to. Then, as time passes, it is more and more difficult to maintain this false image.

Our significant other will start to notice the change in our behavior. Sometimes he or she will consider it as an act of distancing ourselves. So they become more distant as well. Our partner might be in the same boat as us, failing to maintain his or her false image. Thus, the process of distancing described above becomes bidirectional. Each person will start fearing for the relationship; this is when the fear of losing someone steps in.

What do people usually do? They start to keep their opinions to themselves and not talk about problems because, hey, we have enough problems already. They keep a low profile in the relationship with the hope of keeping it together. They avoid confrontation, hiding their true self more than ever before because they don't want to risk separation.

The other behavior end of the spectrum is becoming overly reactive in the relationship. The person who is overly reactive talks about problems all the time, trying to put the blame on the other party. If the other party accepts the reactive person's arguments, he or she can turn into the silent one. Neither of these behaviors is healthy in a relationship and won't bring good results.

The best way to prevent this situation is by not pretending from the start. Let the person who you wish to date know how you really are, what you like, what your values are, and what you dislike. If the two of you are too different, it will show itself. Better sooner than later. If the damage is already done and you presented a false image of yourself, you can still choose to be honest. Then it is up to your partner if he or she wants to continue being with you. Sit down and honestly tell her about the things you pretended to be. You might add that you'd like to work toward becoming the person you pretended to be. This confession is risky, of course, but so is a relationship built on lies.

If you really want a clean slate, you can do it. Let your partner know who you are, and take the unnecessary burden of pretending off your shoulders. The fear of emotional risk will disappear with it.

Fear of confrontation

This type of fear is also rooted in the fear of rejection. We could call it the fear of taking social risks. This fear is triggered by finding yourself in a situation where you have to stand up for yourself and directly confront somebody.

Let's stick to the example of a verbal confrontation, not a physical one. In a verbal showdown the facts and arguments are the weapons. The winner usually is the one with better arguments proven with facts. Let's see the case of taking an intellectual risk.

If you face a biology professor you will probably feel intimidated and afraid to take an intellectual risk. Biology is his field of expertise after all, so trying to outsmart him is risky. This makes sense. It is not fear; it is critical judgment. If you're not at home in biology, you won't risk an argument. You'd probably lose, and you'd be humiliated. You'd probably be reluctant to accept confrontation, even in a field where you have expertise.

But, if you happen to be a biology professor as well, or simply passionate about biology and have been reading about it since childhood, you can give the verbal judo a try. Why? Because you have nothing to lose. If you end up being right, good job. If you lose the argument, you still win by gaining new knowledge and the chance to correct something didn't know. Approach the argument as a listener first, gauge the expertise of the other person, be interested in the other's opinion, and even if it is an argument, try to transform it into a conversation.

Don't give the conversation an edge of confrontation even if you're confident of your knowledge on the topic. It is not necessary to show off. You always have a choice in how you choose to behave. Even if somebody is provoking you to engage in an argument, you can always say, "yes, this is my opinion about the topic, but I'd be very interested in yours. I might be wrong."

Sometimes people engage in really stupid arguments in which they will obviously lose. They are led by negative emotions like anger. After failing, they start complaining about it, blaming everybody and everything.

All these subcategories of fear are rooted in the fear of failure. We're afraid of not being accepted in society — financially, intellectually, or simply as a person by our partner and the people closest to us.

How can you handle them? By doing one thing every day that scares you. There will always be a risk. Always. It takes courage to engage, yes. You may think you don't have enough courage, but you do. In fact, you are the only one who can limit yourself. Raise your limits.

Exercises for this chapter:

1. Take a cold shower today. Do not hesitate to jump into the cold water (unless you have a heart condition that doesn't allow it). After you get used to the cold water, give yourself the comfort of warm water. Do this exercise every day until you're able to step into the cold water without your body and brain screaming STOP and DON'T. Winning against this fear will eventually make the fear vanish.

2. Today I did the following thing that scares me:

Chapter 8: Don't Miss Your Shots

"You'll always miss 100% of the shots you don't take."
--Wayne Gretzky

Don't misunderstand this quote. It doesn't mean you need to say yes and engage in every little thing life throws at you as not to miss out on every opportunity. The quote is talking about missing the real opportunities.

Opportunities are sometimes hard to notice. Why? Because they don't look or sound the way we imagined an opportunity would be presented. Some people want to make more money and only see opportunity as a promotion, a new job at another company, winning the lottery, or getting an inheritance. They may never get one of those opportunities. However, opening a business built on their talent, like painting or woodworking, could have provided them with the desired income if these talents were seen as an opportunity.

We usually have a picture in our mind, an opinion of what an opportunity should look like, and so we wait and wait for this imaginary opportunity to show up – just as we envisioned it. While waiting for the unrealistic to occur, some real diamond in the rough opportunities may pass by us.

Real shots fall into our lap when we least expect them, usually in a shape we didn't think of. Let me share a joke about the material girl and the modest boy.

Material girl: Do you have a BMW?

Modest boy: No, I do not.

Material girl: Do you have a downtown flat?
Modest boy: I do not.
Material girl: Do you have a steady job?
Modest boy: I do not.

Following this discussion the material girl leaves and never reaches out to the modest boy again. The modest boy is puzzled thinking to himself I have a Ferrari, a villa outside LA, and I'm the owner of a company. Why would I need a BMW or a job?

The example is a bit sexist and extreme, but it illustrates the point I'm trying to make. We miss many good opportunities because they don't look exactly as we want them to look.

How many times have you said no to something out of ordinary? An unusual job offer? An invitation to go skydiving? A concert that is not exactly in your usual genre of music? Probably more times than you've said yes. People dream about adventure, money, happiness, and an exciting life full of new experiences, but they don't dare to say yes when these opportunities arise.

"I'd rather have a life of 'oh wells' than 'what ifs'."

--Unknown

Next time you find a new opportunity (an uncommon job offer, an invitation to a place you've never been, a free test drive), don't be quick to say no. Rather ask for time and think about the decision. Do the evaluation from Chapter 2: say yes, wait, or say no. Just remember, do not wait for too long.

it's not necessary to say yes to every small gig because you'll burn out. But make thoughtful decisions about opportunities of real value because they may never come back, at least not in the circumstances in which they were presented the first time. Because we are human, our time is fleeting. We cannot return to the same place at the same time. We'll never be younger than we are in this moment. We'll never feel as we do in this moment. There's a risk in everything, but not in time – you can bet on the time passing and not coming back risk-free.

Saying yes to the big things, the unknown things, and the risky things takes courage and willpower, and gives us the ultimate feeling of being alive. Does it still seem like a bad deal?

Make sure if you delay something, it is for the best reason. For example, if you just broke your leg, you shouldn't go bungee jumping or engage in a cross-country bike trip. But otherwise, if every reasonable condition allows it, why not take the chance?

When I hit a decision roadblock, I make an analysis I call TIME. It stands for Task Importance Measurer, or the four categories of distinction: Top-Priority, Important, Meaningless, and Excludable. The main idea of my TIME method is to rank opportunities or tasks into four groups.

1. **Top-Priority**: Essential, urgent, or never-returning tasks/opportunities. These are once-in-a-lifetime or very important opportunities that can have severe consequences if you don't do them.

2. **Important:** Quite important tasks, but returning opportunities. You should say yes to these only if there is no Top-Priority rated task before it. However, delaying them too much can have negative consequences.
3. **Meaningless:** Tasks/opportunities that sound fun, but if you miss them nothing bad will happen. These are the, "hey, come out to grab a beer," type of invitations. Sometimes you say yes, sometimes no. If you say no too often, your friends will stop asking you out after a time, so there is a minor risk in saying no too often. However, it is enough to participate in this kind of activity once in a while.
4. **Excludable:** Tasks/opportunities that you should avoid. These are the trivial, nonsensically stupid, or dangerous

tasks that would do you more harm than good. At best they are a waste of your time and without benefits.

The TIME method can help you make decisions and keep order in all areas of your life. It saves you TIME, after all. Don't save the good shots and excitements for later. Take advantage of them when they knock on your door if you feel the time is right.

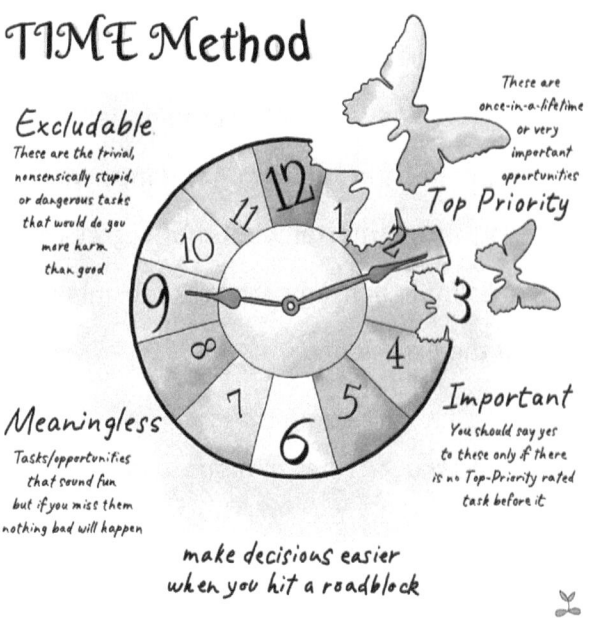

Illustrations by Mixed Media Artist, Karen Dawn For free classes on how to take your learning to a deeper level using creative sketch noting and art journal techniques please www.thevisualjournal.com

Do you have anything to lose?

You'll never find the boundaries of your inner greatness in "no land." You may wake up one day with a mortal wound of regret that is more painful than any scratch you might get during the experience.

"Anyone who has never made a mistake has never tried anything new."

- Albert Einstein

Shots you should miss

There is a new kind of problem human beings are facing in the 21st century: the disease of having too many options. Please be aware of the distinction. Options are not opportunities, but we tend to get them confused. An opportunity is more than an option; opportunities enrich our lives with something long lasting and worthwhile.

Options are simply the freedom to choose one particular thing over something else. It doesn't mean that the chosen option will enrich our lives.

There is a slang term used to define people who confuse opportunities with options and become terrified they are missing out on something in life. This acronym is FOMO: fear of missing out. I will use this acronym from now on.

If you are a millennial or coming from generation z, you have suffered from FOMO at some point in your life. If you are another generation, you may have experienced it, too. I have been going through a FOMO period since I've started traveling.

Whenever I get to a destination, I want to visit everything. If I don't get to visit a particular building, participate in a guided tour, or taste all the special foods, I feel that my travel experience was incomplete and that I did not take full advantage of everything my destination had to offer, despite enjoying my time there.

Every time I ticked a church off my list of must-see things, I would see a picture on Instagram of someone else posing in front of another building that looked much better than than my church. Oh boy! Where was I going to jam that building into my overly packed schedule? I didn't even stop to consider that the Instagram "star" had paid a professional photographer a ridiculous amount of money to take the picture and Photoshop it to the point of it being unrecognizable. No, I needed to see it myself. I needed to take my own picture with my own low-budget camera.

Needless to say, most of my Instagram-inspired photography trips ended in bitter disappointment. My picture was utterly average in comparison because even the building was a letdown without the filters and photo-editing programs to add to its look.

The only thing I achieved was a rushed day at a place I'd paid to visit, but was unable to truly enjoy. I was so fearful of missing out something (not getting a good value from my travel) that I packed the days with activity after activity. In the end, what I ended up missing out on was the purpose of a holiday: relaxation, slowing down, and staying in the present and enjoying the moment.

Luckily, I've realized that my travel plans were driven by FOMO, so I've started to plan my future trips more conscientiously. Today I don't schedule more than two activities a day when I travel, and I stay off Instagram and other influencing social media sites that could disturb my inner peace and push my FOMO button. Thank you for reading about my first world problems that usually happened in the third world.

I gave a lot of thought to the discovery of FOMO in my life because I felt so silly about it. I am so lucky and blessed to be able to visit places I couldn't even dream of a few years ago, but I was ruining the experience for myself. Then I realized that my motivation was misplaced: My main drive wasn't the joy of seeing something amazing, but the fear of not seeing everything amazing.

In other words, today, as a consequence of the fear of missing out, we often work ourselves into a mental state where we are motivated by what we can potentially lose instead of focusing on our gains. But our losses are very often imagined; they are self-invented, self-created, self-torturing thoughts. Do you really think that just because you didn't visit each Trip Advisor suggestion in a particular city that you didn't get to know the place well enough? Or if you don't try each flavor of ice cream that you've missed out something in life?

There is another twist with FOMO, which is also highly enforced with today's social media platforms. While you think that you're missing out on your shots, you simultaneously get the impression that everyone else lives the high life. Look, Mary is in the Bahamas; wow, Jack just had a date with his significant other in Dubai; amazing, Steve just set the Guinness World Record for bungee jumping while painting toenails. Everyone else seems to be going places while you're sitting in your room, cleaning up cat litter.

Having the false belief that everyone else is having more fun can push you to engage in low reward activities, hoping that the next person, travel destination, or experience will be the one that will make your life amazing. So you'll find yourself going out with people you hardly know and feeling insecure because there isn't much chemistry or history between you, and then you'll check Facebook and see your friend, Greg, is at another party across town that is probably is way cooler than one you're at.

We are the luckiest generation who has ever lived because, relatively speaking, there are the least amount of wars, sickness, and famine going on in the world.[ii] We also have more choice, which paradoxically, makes us unhappier than ever before. The phenomenon has earned the name "the paradox of choice" for a reason.

Let's see an example. If you have only eggs and milk in your fridge, you'll make scrambled eggs, eat it, and be happy about it as you move on with your day. But if you go out to have brunch somewhere where they have five types of salami sandwiches with cottage cheese, blue cheese, goat cheese, muesli, yogurt, bacon, cereal, three types of milk, and six kinds of coffee to choose from, it will become overwhelming to choose what to eat and what to ditch. You only have one stomach after all. Even if you succeed at choose something, you'll be thinking about the flavors of the missed options for hours to come. So you pledge to return to this restaurant and try the goat cheese next time. But this is like the twentieth place you wish to go back to, so you start feeling anxious about how you can jam all the amazing food options restaurants have to offer into your life?

The problem with the fear of missing out is that while its purpose is to enrich your life with experience, in reality it rather keeps you from meaningful moments. Your brain will be always spinning on the next best thing instead of focusing on the best thing of the present. There will always be a nicer, cooler, sexier, wealthier option around the corner than what you have at the moment.

The question is when will you be able to stop, honestly say that enough is enough, and start to enjoy what you have in the moment? Real life is not always full of green fields, blue beaches, thin girls, or muscular men as the illusion of future experiences promise. But we both know that all that glitters is not gold. Certainly, social media is good at showing off the glitter, but it bitterly misses out on showing the realities of life.

Did you identify with the fear of missing out? Now are you wondering how you can escape from its vicious circle? Let go of the impression of perfection; stop believing your fantasies. You will never have a perfect trip or a perfect husband or a perfect work environment. There will always be bumps in the road, What makes life good or bad is relative and bound to be unpredictable. For example, you could go to Bali to have the time of your life right after your wife leaves you, but you'll still feel miserable.

In life, everything has a payoff. The truth is, sometimes it is better not to pay the literal or figurative price for some things. There is an opportunity cost for everything. Staying home often is better than going out. While it is true that you physically miss out on an event, in reality you won't miss out on anything.

I just arrived home in Timisoara, the town where my parents live, a few days ago after traveling for six months. While I had visited some of the most amazing places on Earth, I realized I had still missed out on things.

I had given up the warmth and unconditional love of my parents and closest friends. I had ceased being present in my home community and my relationships with some people weakened. I have never felt so protected and cherished anywhere in the world as here. There is no place like home, indeed. This being said, I don't regret traveling. Meaning comes in many forms in life. Some are food for the soul, others are food for Instagram and Pinterest.

The bottom line, we are always missing out on something, it doesn't matter what we do. The most valuable experiences in life can't be seen. Learning something new, loving someone deeply, the feeling of belonging somewhere will always beat the palm trees and glitter. At some point you'll realize as I did that life doesn't get richer by collecting more experience, things, or people, but by learning to focus and be content with less.

Exercises for this chapter:

1. Today I said yes to this opportunity:

   ……………………………………………………………
…………………………………………………………

2. Saying yes to the opportunity above turned out to be:

   ……………………………………………………………
…………………………………………………………

3. Today I defeated the urge to do this out of FOMO:

   ……………………………………………………………
…………………………………………………………

Chapter 9: Start By Doing What's Necessary

"Start by doing what's necessary, then do what's possible, suddenly you are doing the impossible."
                              --St. Francis of Assisi

I don't know if you realized, but the exercises and advice in this book don't cost any money. Their success only depends on the effort and time you invest. Write every "Today I…" exercise on a separate paper and randomly pick at least one to practice each day. You can make this practice a fun game. Put each paper in a hat and just pull one out every morning. Leave the one you picked outside the hat to avoid repeating the same exercise. When every paper is out of the hat, put them back and start pulling out the papers again from the start.

For example, say you pick "Today I will do something that scares me." This has to be an easy one since we have so many fears and so many things seem terrifying to us. Sometimes even talking to someone, trying out a bright lipstick or commuting on public transport can be scary. Just do something that scares you. Do not delay by saying, *Oh, I would like to talk to Bill from accounting, but he probably won't even reply to me*. This is an excuse. Do you really think that Bill is such a schmuck that he wouldn't even reply? Why would you want to talk to him in the first place if that was the case? I'm sure Bill is a nice person who is just as scared of rejection as you are. Just take a deep breath, say hi to him, and ask him something accounting-related to create rapport. If you like Bill, it is necessary to start to build a relationship somewhere. Start there, at a simple hi.

If you wish to learn to wear more vivid makeup, it is necessary to start somewhere. Start at an orange or deep purple lipstick. If you wish to ditch road rage and getting stuck in the morning traffic, give to public transportation a chance. Guess who's riding it? People. Human beings like you and me. I've met the most interesting people in my life riding the bus, the train, or the subway.

Making a change starts with one step; usually stepping on our fear, prejudice or judgment. Courage is built upon these small steps.

If you think that setting big goals is harder, you're wrong. For most people it's actually easier. The lofty, impossible goals people seem to promise themselves are little more than mere wishes. They never actually commit to them. Deep down, they know they won't accomplish these goals, but since they sound good, they set them anyway. It's a clever way to create a machine of excuses. With a real challenge, these people will always have something to complain about, and unfortunately, they will believe that their complaints are legitimate.

My dad is a perfect example of this kind of attitude. He always shoots for the brightest star: to drive a Jaguar, to buy a wood cabin on a fishing lake… But he has had no income in years. When people suggest that he start dreaming for the average Romanian salary, he shouts out in anger, saying that people have killed his vision. His favorite scapegoats are the Romanian political system, the holidays that sabotage him from making money, and the people whose mindset is not ready for what he's trying to deliver. He is full of excuses as to why he is unsuccessful in a business that he has run for almost fifteen years. His perseverance is admirable. Not many people would try and fail in the same thing for fifteen years and still do it with the same enthusiasm. Albert Einstein's definition of insanity is "doing the same thing over and over and expecting different results."

Don't be like my dad. Perseverance and belief in oneself are very important qualities, but be observant and notice when they are not put to work for the achievable goal. If my dad is right, and he is just rounding the last corner to finally achieve his long-awaited success, I'll make sure to update this book. But even if that happens, instead of waiting more than fifteen years to succeed, choose a different path.

Set risky, fear-defeating but achievable goals. Instead of wishing for a Jaguar, just aim to buy yourself a reliable second hand car of any kind. Use this car to create more income by saving time on travel, driving it as an Uber – you name it. Then upgrade it to another car. And another. If you work smart, you'll have your Jaguar, and suddenly you are doing the impossible. [iii]

Set goals that you are able to believe in. Every goal is achievable but not without a strong belief in your ability to make it happen. How do you get this belief? Through practice. Think of it as the same as building a muscle: The more time you achieve a difficult, but achievable goal, the more this muscle will strengthen. One day the goal that seemed so difficult and impossible to believe in will be at your feet.

Take the initiative to work on your problems. Don't wait until life kicks you out of your comfort zone. The habit of showing initiative is a quality that will make you distinguishable in any community. Take the initiative by planning to do what's necessary and possible, and then finish the tasks related to them as quickly and efficiently as possible.

Very few people are masters of task completion. But research has proven that taking responsibility and making a habit of doing tasks quickly are qualities of successful people. You can make sure to complete your tasks following these steps:

1. Choose something you want to do today. You can pick an exercise from this book, but you can also make one up to meet your needs. Let's stick with the previous example: *today I will do*

something that scares me. I chose defeating the fear of heights for this exercise.

2. Divide a piece of paper into three columns and write on the top of each column: Necessary – Possible – Impossible.

3. Divide the first two columns (necessary and possible) into five to ten sections. Leave the third as a full column.

4. Select some activity related to the chosen fear – the fear of heights in my case - you consider to be impossible. For example: *I want to skydive*.

5. Work often on your fear of heights. Do something that closes the gap between

your current fear and skydiving. Fill in the first two columns with the necessary and possible steps you make to fulfill your 'impossible goal.'. You can also add the date to each occasion so you can track how much time has passed since you pledged to reach your impossible goal. Give yourself a reasonable deadline. To get used to the idea of skydiving, and making preparations for trying it, one month should be a reasonable time.

6. If five to ten occasions aren't enough to get to the impossible goal, extend your chart a few more steps. Be careful to not delay your impossible goal on purpose.

	Necessary	Possible	Impossible
4th June	Go to town.	Climb to the highest floor of the tallest building.	**Skydiving!!**
13th June	Go to the amusement park.	Take a round on the Ferris wheel.	
21st June	Find alternatives to skydiving.	Try indoors skydiving for example.	
28th June	Go to the countryside.	Try paragliding.	
1st July	Take a free day.	Go to the closest skydive place.	

The chart above should give you an idea of how to work step by step toward an impossible goal. As you can see you don't have to work on the same fear every day. Just track your progress toward reaching your impossible goal, make sure not to procrastinate, and you'll see that one day, you'll do the impossible just by following some small, necessary steps.

Exercise of the day:

1. Today I made the chart for ……………………….. and I did …………………….. as the step of necessity and ……………………… as the possible step.

2. Today I did something that a ………. (month, week, year) ago I considered impossible……………………………………………
…………

Chapter 10: Unlearning Versus Learning

"Unlearning is more difficult than learning."
--English Proverb

Illustrations by Mixed Media Artist, Karen Dawn For free classes on how to take your learning to a deeper level using creative sketch noting and art journal techniques please www.thevisualjournal.com

Our life is a long learning process. We learn to walk, to talk, to write, and to count. Later we learn about history, geography, human relations, literature, and chemistry and all the things they teach us in conventional education.

There is, however, another, more indirect learning channel: the deep-burning effect of repeated actions that we call habits. Habitual learning is not conscious. We just do certain things, and after a time, we treat them as our standard way of being or thinking. Needless to say, the majority of people believe more in the negative things.

- I'm not a good swimmer.
- I'm not a people person.
- I'm bad at math.

The list of our ironclad negative beliefs is endless. Still, believing the negative is only one bad habit, even if it has many shades. We learn other harmful habits in our life, like self-hatred, self-directed negative criticism, and others. But here's the key: we learn them. As Newton's third law says, "For every action, there is an equal and opposite reaction." Just as we have learned these habits, we can unlearn them.

The unlearning process, however, can prove to be more difficult than the learning process because we've learned the bad habit unconsciously, starting in childhood, and that means we've had ten, twenty, thirty years of active unconscious practice.

Unlearning these bad habits requires awareness, focus, and conscious practice. And yes, it will take some time too. Ideally not as much as it took to learn them, but I don't want to lie and say you can get rid of a twenty-year-long bad habit overnight. You developed your habit in response to stimuli from a young age. Even if the unlearning process takes a long time, there are practices that can help speed it up.

One of the most famous experiments on classical conditioning – conditioned reflex specifically - was Ivan Pavlov's. In this experiment, he mixed a dog's biological stimulus with a previously neutral one. Every time the dog was fed, Pavlov rang a bell before feeding the dog. The animal got used to this system of feeding. After a while, Pavlov would ring the bell, but didn't offer any food. However, the sound of the bell itself elicited the physical reflex of salivation in the dog. [iv]

You can develop a similar conditioning pattern regarding your bad habits in the following ways:

a.) Ask your friends to, whenever they see, hear, or feel you doing the bad habit, do something very specific like pinch your arm, shake you, or just say an uncommon relatable sentence. For example, I tend to get angry and hyper-analyze why my boyfriend said (or didn't say) something. I share almost everything with my dad. He's my best friend. So when he notices that I'm going down that rabbit hole of nonsensical analysis again, he just says, "Your brain is being eaten by the brain-eater bug from Madagascar again."

Yes, you read that correctly. I feel the same way about it, and I have a Windows Blue Screen of Death/restart moment to process what he just said. Then I start laughing because it's such a stupid and funny thing to say. That gets me out of my angry thought spiral instantly. I've told my friends about this "bug" too, so now when I start the unnecessary thinking, they tell me and I stop instantly. These days when I get angry, I recall this Madagascar bug even when I'm alone, and then I slowly calm down.

b.) The other thing you can do is practice doing the opposite of your habit at certain times of the day. For example, let's say you often talk or think negatively about yourself and you want to change that. Set an alarm on your phone to five different times a day. Every time you hear the alarm, say or think something good, encouraging, or mood lifting about yourself.

You will see that after a while, even if you don't hear the alarm, you'll recognize when the time has come to do your "task." You can connect this process to a secondary neutral stimulus, which is time, too. So if your alarm rang for half a year every day at noon, let's say, even if you turn the alarm off, you'll still remember at noon that you have a task to do.

This reversed conditioning can be used to leave behind physical bad habits as well. I was not hydrating myself well. I set an alarm for six times a day and every time it rang, I drank a glass of water. This was a while ago, and I don't have the alarms anymore, but my body is so used to drinking water at those times that I feel thirsty a few moments before my alarm would have sounded. Now I drink automatically. Now that I mention it... I think I need to drink my water.

Develop new habits

Instead of sweating your heart out to get rid of a bad habit, develop a good habit. Fill your day with practicing the consciously chosen good habit so you won't have as much time to do your bad ones.

Many of us are willing to change and leave bad habits behind when something terrible happens. Sometimes we need a shock to consider getting rid of a bad habit. My uncle, who used to be a chain smoker, quit smoking the day his father, my grandfather, died. Losing his father unexpectedly made him value life more, so he gave up on his vicious habit. But do we need to wait for such extreme events to improve our lives?

If we condition ourselves differently, we don't have to wait for a shock to prompt our change in behavior. We'll be more eager to change if we stop focusing on leaving bad behavior behind, which is a long and difficult process, and focus on learning a positive new one. Some scientists say it takes twenty-one to twenty-eight days to develop a new habit. Regardless if these numbers are accurate or not, we have nothing to lose if we try to develop a new habit that is the opposite of our negative one.

It's all about marketing. I read about an experiment conducted among high school students. They were taking a test. Half the class was told that the test was difficult and that many people might fail. The other half was told that the test was easy-peasy and a chance for students to earn an extra A before the end of the school year. The kids who believed the test was easy, got As and Bs. However, three-quarters of the kids who were told it was hard earned below a C. Some kids with low confidence and historically bad grades didn't even read the exercises. They handed a blank test because they believed so deeply in their incompetence.

This example proves that very often the key to achievement is not coded in our abilities but in our belief in our abilities.

When people have a big aha moment about what they're doing wrong, they become enthusiastic about change. Suddenly they want to change everything – their relationships, work, morals, world view, daily routines, eating habits… Everything.

But this over-fueled enthusiasm collapses quite quickly. Usually at the first opportunity they revert to their bad habits. Then the brain-munching bug arises, *who am I trying to fool? I can't change.* They would be able to change if they took small, step-by-step goals, but they fail and give up instead because they tried to bite off more than they could chew. Setting multiple big goals (changing one's ingrained behavior is a big goal) at once leaves a lot of room for error, failure, and thus a reinforced belief in ones incapability to change.

In my experience, you can't handle more than two to three new habits at once. Also, try to choose the new habits in the same life area. For example, if you want to be more athletic, set three new habits in that domain. Waking up earlier, going for a run, and having a less carb-filled diet is plenty of change to handle. If you wish to make changes in your working attitude as well, wait until your new workout-nutrition routine becomes effortless.

Waking up early and doing more physical exercise, not to mention ditching afternoon binging, deplete your willpower badly enough. If you try working hard during this period, chances are that you'll give in to afternoon binging. Once you mess up your diet, you'll give in to sleeping more because who cares, you already won't achieve your fitness goal. More sleep means less exercise or no exercise. Failing to stick with one good habit will make you depressed, so you won't be able to focus on your work as well. So you'll binge even more. And voilà, the vicious circle of too many changes just closed.

Don't worry. You can become the person of your dreams - just not immediately. Don't overestimate what can you do in the short term, but don't underestimate the things you can achieve long-term. Patience, my friend. Work hard, focus, and change not more than two to three things at a time.

Exercises for this chapter:

1. Today I did this to develop these two new habits:

   ....

   ....

2. Due to my new good habits I started unlearning this bad habit:

   ....

   ....

Chapter 11: Curiosity Will Conquer

> *"Curiosity will conquer fear even more than bravery will."*
> --James Stephens

As a kid you saw everything as an adventure. You were fearless, not overwhelmed by thoughts of *whats* and *ifs* and *what will they think?* What was the mindset that drew you toward adventures?

Curiosity.

As adults we can distinguish between good and bad, safety and danger. But where is the thin line between being cautious and overly cautious? What is the force that kills curiosity?

Are you a person who often says, *be careful*, *it's too risky*, or *it's too dangerous?* Did you become the I-don't-have-time machine who got trapped in the I-have-to-work-to-buy-food-to-have-strength-to-work cycle? All of us need to work for food, there's no problem with that. But we have other needs we should consider after our stomach is full. We nee food for the soul. Living only for routines makes our happiness and excitement tank empty.

The fear of judgment, displeasure, and criticism often hold us back and prevent us to do anything different than "normal." Break the chains of monotony! There's always something at risk, better accept it. Whether you're risking your good reputation, your money, your time, health, or relationships, there is no greater danger than plodding through life without living it.

Unleash your curiosity. If curiosity is followed by action, it automatically fills you with courage, self-trust, and fulfillment from the discovery. True confidence is having the courage to consider yourself worthy of exploring and living life to the fullest.

You are like a bottomless lake; you'll always be able to discover new depths of your character you didn't even know you had. Do not be afraid to face your interests and ask the question of "why didn't I do this earlier?" Yes, you might realize that you wasted some time repressing the curious kid within you, but that time is history. What's still ahead of you is a mystery. Are you curious to know how you will unfold?

Who are you? What drives you? What are you after? What's preventing you from getting it? What's your deepest wound?

What's your greatest pride? Do you know the answers to these questions? Are you curious? The answers are in you. Just take the time to answer them.

Unleash your social curiosity. When you're satisfied with your own personal discovery, take your curiosity to the next level. Satisfy your social curiosity. I bet you are curious about what's going on with other people, even if you try to convince yourself that you are not. Talking about each other was an essential tool our hunter-gatherer ancestors used to make good decisions. Through this information exchange, they knew who was a trustworthy person, who was lazy, who was good at fighting, who would be a reliable hunter or gatherer, who had bad breath, who was evil, and so on. These were important factors to know back then and they are important today too. Talking about our peers is ingrained in our nature. But it is only useful when we talk about true facts. Spreading untrue information about other people is gossiping. That's a different story.

Sometimes people get so trapped in their lives and problems that they forget there is a world full of other people out there. Speaking with others boosts not only your social confidence, but also helps you realize that you are not alone in your struggles.

How can you approach others with curiosity? Remember when you were a kid and thought astronauts were the coolest thing ever? Try to capture that feeling and think of the people around you as astronauts. Consider everybody to be interesting because they are. Everyone has a few cool stories to share or thoughtful ideas to spread. So, as a kid, what would you have liked to ask an astronaut?

Don't expect others to be interesting. Show genuine interest, and they will prove to be worthy of your curiosity. People like to talk about themselves and explain their inner motivations. Your curiosity will make them feel important, and in exchange, you'll get attention too, which yes, will boost your sense of importance and confidence. There is a reason why humans are called social beings.

Sure enough, there are very self-absorbed people who only talk about themselves without returning the attention. You're free to not invest more time in such people anytime you choose. The majority of people, however, are not like that. So don't give up on humanity just because of a few bad examples.

Ask ask ask. Don't stop at asking surface questions. Ask everything you want to know about the other person. Once you feel the relationship is at that point, dig deeper, not wider, into the other person's heart. The most interesting conversations are never the ones about favorite actors, restaurants, or places to visit. They are more about the hidden reasons why the actor, restaurant, or place is important to someone.

Don't be shy or afraid to ask about technical things you don't know. There's a Chinese proverb that says a person who asks stays stupid for five minutes, and a person who doesn't ask stays stupid all his life. Don't be afraid to ask the most obvious questions without feeling foolish. What if you know nothing about baseball? Who cares? Questions will show that you're genuinely interested in the other person, his or her expertise, or stories.

Life has proved to me again and again

that the dumb and obvious questions are the ones I should ask most of the time. They bring clarity. Saying "I don't understand" either drives people crazy and they leave you (thus you will know that this person is not interested in helping you) or leads you to a lot of useful information. Either way, you're better informed. So why not ask more questions?

Exercises for this chapter:

1. Three things I was curious about as a kid:

I.
....
....
II.
....
....

III.

....

....

2. Three things I wish I'd done differently in the past ten years:

I.

....

....

II.

....

....

III.

....

....

3. Three things that I'm curious about today:

I.

....
....

II.

....
....

III.

....
....

4. One action I can do TODAY to satisfy my curiosity:.

....
....

Chapter 12: Life After Success

"A hard fall means a high bounce ... if you're made of the right material."

— Unknown Author

Illustrations by Mixed Media Artist, Karen Dawn For free classes on how to take your learning to a deeper level using creative sketch noting and art journal techniques please www.thevisualjournal.com

By this point, I've talked about how to achieve success, how to go through the pitfalls of everyday life challenges to get your dream job, your dream girl or guy, your dream house full of cats, and other subjects. The book presented how to stay resilient, how to be brave, and how to set and achieve small and seemingly impossible goals in life.

But what happens after success is achieved?

This is the question I ponder the most, these days. As a writer, I have my cherished little dreams about getting to the top of the *New York Times* bestseller list one day, selling millions of copies of my book worldwide, and getting lots of feedbacks from readers saying, "Thank you, Zoe, you really helped me." I still haven't achieved this dream, but I've already ticked off some milestones in my writing career plan. I hit the number one position in the Amazon Author Ranking for Health, Fitness and Dieting category. One of my books made it to the top 500 overall book ranking.

Weirdly, I don't really feel anything about these accomplishments. Ticking off these milestones doesn't fill me with the contentment I was expecting to experience in the planning phase. I was so excited to plan my milestones, to work to my best ability and create quality work deserving of success. The road was bumpy. I was getting good and bad feedback, but finally, I reached some goals I had set for myself. If success means reaching our goals again and again, I can say I'm successful. But am I really?

Every milestone reached, every step ticked, takes me to a dilemma deeply rooted in fear. Namely, how will I top this?

I mean neither to brag, nor complain when I talk about my career as a writer. I want to point out that success brings people to new roadblocks, new fears, and new challenges.

Every time I start pondering what my next book should be about, I can't help comparing my idea to my most successful books. I'm full of doubt and fear whether or not I've reached the limit of my potential. What ifs invade my head. The feeling of success certainly gives me peace of mind and a sense of accomplishment. But it also results in new psychological fallouts.

Everyone who experiences success in their lives probably faces the shadowed side of success too. Namely, the more successful you become, the higher your expectations will rise — not only expectations toward yourself, but also your expectations of others and life in general. If you hit 100 once, hitting only 90 the next time would seem like a failure. The higher you set your expectations, the greater the risk that you'll fail to meet them. If we can believe the saying, "The lower your expectations, the happier you'll be," guess what happens in this case?

The irony of this situation is that your fears and insecurities are not created by failures, but by the success you've craved for so long.

Fear generated by your own success is a dangerous pitfall. Why? Because it can kick you into the deep pit of self-doubt. "Will I be able to create something better than that, or should I stop on the top of the mountain before I fall down?" Or it may lead you to perfectionism. "I need to be the best now. I have a reputation to live up to. Mistakes are not permitted, or people will think I lost my fire."

Have you ever felt this feeling?

This chapter talks about the problems of those who crave creativity and are up working more and harder for additional success. These people simply hit a mental roadblock of insecurity. They experience the other side of the equation. They become discouraged on a different level than before.

Before they achieved success, they courageously jumped on the road of their dreams knowing they had nothing to lose by trying. What's the worst-case scenario? They fail. So what? They start over or quit. But when they create something, they succeed in something, and suddenly there is something to lose — their reputation, their position, their level of income. After success the stakes are higher. Failure demands a bigger price to pay.

I can imagine your face darkening as you read my words, if you consider yourself currently successful and you fight with these demons, and if you still wish to conquer the Mount Olympus of your goals. Worry not, my friend. Insecurities following success are not as bad as they seem, although they can be quite torturous.

What you need to overcome them is courage.

Not the kind of courage you needed in the beginning of your journey, but a different one. Courage to accept that *success is not linear*.

"Yesterday's maximum is today's minimum."

— Quote on my gym's wall by an Unknown Author

I have a conflicted relationship with this quote. It used to be a great motivation in my life, up to a point — the point where I experienced some success. Then it became more like a burden to carry. Each day I didn't exceed the success of the day before, I went to bed disappointed. Each day I exceeded the success of the day before, I went to bed terrified by what the next day might hold.

One day, I decided to stop depending on the message of that stupid quote. I tried to convince myself that I didn't care about my success dilemma anymore. However, I couldn't forget this quote and kept brainstorming about its message until I realized that I've misunderstood the message of the quote all along. I always thought that the quote, and success in general, was measured by the result. But I was wrong.

The quote's message, just like success, is measured in the input.

It turns out the cliché is true: Happiness in life is about the journey, not the destination. If you focus on the destination of "yesterday's maximum, today's minimum," sooner or later, you'll fail bitterly. There is only a certain amount of time, energy, talent you can invest in something to get better results each day. If you focus on your efforts to be the "yesterday's maximum, today's minimum," you'll always be fulfilled. Do just one percent more than the day before to become better at what you do.

Don't measure your success by the outcome. It is about the effort, hard work, diligence, and resilience you put into your work. It is easy to work hard while you're starving. But working hard when you could dine like a French king, that's the true willpower.

Many of us assume, myself included, that just because in the beginning any successful journey is, indeed, linear, it should and will always be so. This is a mistake. After the first few miles, the first thousand readers, achievements will inevitably vary, partly because you can't control the outcome in most professions, and partly because this is the nature of work — especially creative work.

Let me ask you this: if you had a breakthrough success, let's say you sold 1,000 photos of your scrambled eggs in one month and only 500 in the next — would the success of the first month diminish the success of the second one?

Or are both of them great achievements as they are — uniquely? You did your job diligently. You made the scrambled eggs, you took the photos, and you sold them, improving your presentation technique in the meantime. That is success.

A Paradox Within Another Paradox

The paradox of success is that the more successful you become, the less secure you feel, and the more compelled you are to outdo your present success with future ones. This paradox leads to another paradox: The more insecure you feel about future successes, the more challenging your activities should be.

"Like I don't feel challenged enough already," you might growl now.

Being challenged by expectations and being overwhelmed by them is not the same thing. Expectations put pressure on you, while challenges inspire. Instead of forcing yourself to constantly outdo your previous success, focus instead on achieving the same thing using alternative routes. This might sound counterintuitive at first. It may sound like you should get stuck on a level of success and never try to step above it, just circle around it aimlessly. I certainly don't want to suggest this. You should aim to create the best possible outcome for whatever you're working on. Just don't make your success, happiness, and self-worth dependent on it. Just because one day you make less, get endorsed less than another day, it doesn't mean the day was a failure or that you'll never top your best achievement ever again.

Insecurity needs new soils to grow. Insecurity triggered by success isn't the type of insecurity you feel when you haven't accomplished anything. This insecurity knows that you are able. That's why it is so critical to challenge yourself.

If you've met all the challenges of your current goals, continuing to work at the same challenge level or level of quality could become too easy. In other words, it will lose its challenging aspect and you might end up bored or stuck in a rut. If you feel bored when writing a book, for example, the reader will be even more so. Routine requires a lot of knowledge, that's for sure, but it kills the sense of challenge.

Ultimately, even the most creative, innovative work becomes boring after a while. People who work in the same field for a decade or more know what I'm talking about.

When I became a writer, the most exciting thing about it was avoiding the repetition of a regular job, to be constantly challenged and creative. Joke's on me. I'm doing the same thing day-by-day, every day. At the beginning of my writing career, I thought I was a special little snowflake doing something earth-shatteringly unique. The realization of how average my life actually is makes me smile. In general, the human experience is more universal than it seems. Accepting my own averageness made me less cocky, and at the same time, released a lot of pressure. I don't feel the need to prove myself in numbers anymore.

Today, I want to keep myself challenged for the sake of daily improvement. I want to improve my writing style, deepen my thoughts, express them better, and read better stories to make my books more and more enjoyable for readers. I'm ready to accept that success might not show in numbers, I might not conquer my highest mountain tomorrow, but I will be satisfied to know that I put more than my best knowledge in my work.

The main takeaway of this chapter is to embrace insecurity born from success, keep it challenged, and focus on improving yourself to meet your next milestone, instead of getting depressed if the milestone is not immediately met. Just like in video games, reaching the next level always requires more skills, more patience, and more time. While advancing from level one to five was a piece of cake, doing the same five-level advancement between level thirty and level thirty-five might take years. As long as you find the journey challenging, you'll go on.

Exercises for This Chapter:

1. Three ways I can challenge myself to achieve everyday success:

I.

....
....

II.

....
....

III.

....
....

2. Three reasons why the insecurity I feel due to success is better than the insecurity I felt before success:

I.

....
....

II.

III.

Chapter 13: Courage To Accept Mediocrity

"When your dreams turn to dust, vacuum."

— Unknown Author

When you daydream about your future success, your often picture it as a rosy transition from rookie to rock star that involves a lot of joy, occasional graceful failures making you more respectful, and high-fiving hundreds of people at a stadium in which you're performing the best show of your life.

But in reality, great successes are usually triggered by trauma or an extreme negative event in one's life — losing your income source, a divorce, a failed business, or the death of a loved one. Trauma and failure force you to slow down in whatever you're doing, take a step back, and contemplate your deepest values and motivations in life. In the best case, after a big fall, you get yourself together and put your head into some real work. In the worst case, you dig yourself even deeper into pain.

Let's be optimistic and say you put all your best effort in achieving your goal. You gracefully fail and are reborn as a phoenix, rising gloriously from the ashes. You face all the traumas, fight all the odds that are between you and your dreams, and the hardship of life doesn't get you. Still, against all your best efforts and heroism, the most you can achieve is a mediocre result.

Why? Because like it or not, most of us were not born to be exceptional — regardless of what today's if-you-can-dream-it-you-can-do-it culture or your mom told you. This sounds depressing and you might start to hate me, but let me elaborate on this thought and you'll see it is not so bad.

If you paid even minimal attention in statistics (and you survived it with a sane mind), you might have heard of the bell curve. The bell curve, so aptly named for the is a bell-shaped, convex curve of data points on a graph. Let's put all seven billion people on the planet on the vertical side of the graph, and below-average, average, and above-average characteristics on the horizontal side.

On the ascending twenty percent of the curve are the people who have below-average skills at a random craft — let's say painting. On the descending twenty percent of the curve are the people who are true artists. In the midsection, sixty percent of the bell curve are people who are simply average at painting.

Let's pick a painter — let's say Claude Monet (my favorite). He was a painting genius. If I had to position him on our imaginary bell curve of painting skills, he'd be somewhere at the very tip of the right, descending side, in the top one percent of people with above-average painting skills.

If we take the unknown tattoo artist who is responsible for the disaster, we can

agree that he has below-average painting (and drawing) skills.

Probably a half-armed monkey could draw a better picture, but certainly most of us would. We are all mesmerized by the legacy of Monet, and we laugh about this guy with a horrible tattoo of… a panther? But the truth is, we'll probably never be either of them.

We all have strengths and weaknesses. But at the end of the day, on a worldwide scale, most of us are quite average at most things we do. Even Tiger Woods, who is an exceptional golfer, may only be average at cooking, soccer, or drawing. And that's perfectly fine. Nobody aims for mediocrity, which is also good. Trying to get ahead in life having mediocre goals won't challenge you enough. But accepting that you can't be exceptional at everything is a healthy way to approach life.

There are so few of us who are willing to accept our average awesomeness. People revolt, they start dwelling in their offended ego, screaming about how special they are, how much they deserve excellence. But to become above-average at something, you have to invest a lot of time and energy into it. Even to excel at only one thing might take a lifetime of work. And because we are limited in time and energy, only some people, like Arnold Schwarzenegger, will be really outstanding at more than one thing. Even for him it took a lifetime to master bodybuilding, acting, and politics. And he is definitely the exception, not the rule. For each Picasso, Dostoyevsky, and Michael Phelps, there are hundreds of millions of … us. Regardless of how we grind, some of us won't get there. This doesn't mean that our life is worthless and we should hole up playing videogames until we die. In fact, this means we are normal human beings.

Accepting our own mediocrity doesn't mean that we should give up on our dreams. Nobody knows who will be the lucky upper twenty percent. We should strive to be our best selves each day, and go for what we dream, fight and win and laugh and cry and be okay with who we are. I know it has never been harder to be okay with mediocrity. Having access to technology and social media exposes us to unrealistic expectations. Everything memorable we read about or see presents the extremes of the bell curve. Why? Because extreme good and extreme bad are what makes the headlines.

Our attention, however, is limited. So only those things that are exceptionally good or bad leak into our brains — the best models, the best diet, the best car, the funniest people, the richest ones, etc. As a consequence, our sense of reality gets so distorted that we start to believe that real life looks like those extremes. When real life truly happens in the sixty percent of the bell curve.

Once I was fantasizing of writing a script for a movie that presents a couple's life after the big romance part is over — a movie that would show the regular, everyday life of people who love each other and have no problems apart from the regular ones. No young blonde in the picture, no tripods invading the earth, no daughter getting kidnapped. Just an average life. My argument for this movie was to show a good example of relationships to the generation that grew up on Disney and *Titanic*. When I presented my idea to my boyfriend, he promptly talked me out of it by saying, "No one would buy or watch such a movie. No one cares about average."

He's right. No one does, even though our lives, and the lives of the celebrities we follow on Instagram, are composed of mostly average events. Still, since our attention is constantly grabbed by extraordinary events, we ended up believing that is the new normal. Therefore, anytime when we're not experiencing exceptional circumstances (ninety-nine percent of the time), we end up thinking something's wrong with us. We start feeling insecure about ourselves. We feel pressure to prove our specialness. The main aim is to be different than the rest of society, no matter what. This is a psychological byproduct of our society today, and it is not a good one.

The cruelest joke of today's exceptionalism is that even exceptional people are totally forgettable. Some practice their craft for long years, investing a lot of money and hours to capture their excellence on a camera to show the world. You get those five seconds of exhilaration when you watch the video, and five minutes later, you're hooked on the next video. For example, you can watch a professional surfer flawlessly riding a huge wave and start feeling jealous, thinking, "Oh, that's so cool. I'd never be able to do that." Then, supporting your head with one hand, you scroll down on your Reddit feed and stumble upon another video about a bear tamer who makes the bear jump and dance. By this moment, the surfer is long forgotten.

As you can see, there is a competition even in the field of excellence. While individually, the surfer and the bear tamer do some amazingly unique stuff, being thrown together into the deep ocean of the Internet, their performances become fodder for the online populous. If everybody is exceling, nobody is.

People fear accepting mediocrity because they believe that's the route to living an unsuccessful and sad life. There are some hidden problems in thoughts like this. Namely, if you think that only an exceptional life is a worthy life, you basically consider most peoples' lives unworthy. Think about it — is that really true? Are peoples' lives unworthy, sad, and boring just because they don't live like Kylie Jenner?

People who reach the above-average level of excellence are also average people, just focused. They don't think they are that special; they just become obsessed with something deeper than the rest of us and are willing to devote their life to that purpose. What you can't see on social media is that they hardly ever go out for a beer with friends. They eat protein bars and weird food every day. They train and practice when you're watching Netflix and sipping tea. True achievers constantly feel they are average or below average, and this notion pushes them to improve more and more.

Let me tell you a secret: As soon as you take a deep breath, gather the courage to tell yourself, "Yes, I'm average, but that's just normal and I'm still worthy and capable of a happy life," a lot of pressure will leave your system. You'll get rid of that excruciating compulsion to become more and more for the sake of putting on a show. You'll accept who you are and focus on being the best version of yourself. And while focusing on your own stuff, striving to be better than the day before, you might peak in some areas and get those fifteen minutes of fame. When you walk toward your goal because it gives you pleasure instead of being dragged by expectations, you'll feel much happier and fulfilled, regardless of the outcome.

Slowly, you'll learn to appreciate the proverbial small things in life like the security of a good friendship, making someone happy, helping a person in need, laughing with your love, reading something exciting, or eating a great Italian gelato. None of the events above would earn a thousand likes, and yet life makes the most sense during these moments.

Exercises for This Chapter:

1. Today, I accepted my mediocrity in this field:

   ……………………………………………………………
   …………………………………………………………

2. Today, I valued the simple beauty of this event that I took for granted previously:

....

....

Final Words

"Life is either a daring adventure or nothing."
--Helen Keller

A life well lived doesn't come by blindly following some self-help mojos or faking it till you make it, but by the courage to live a life of adventures.

If I could summarize the best of my experiences for you, I'd say this:
- Food never tastes as great as when you're hungry.
- Your loved ones' touch never feels as good as when you've been without it.
- Christmases don't hold the meaning of spending happy time with your family

until you've spent the holidays without them.
- Winning doesn't feel as dear as when you've failed at least once before seizing it.
- You can't live a life of adventure until you've experienced how empty life can be without it.

It doesn't matter how tall you are, how wealthy you are, the color of your skin, your religious beliefs, or who you love. These things are not the primary qualities that define what kind of person you are. I've seen generous rich people and churchgoers being stingy with the needy. I've seen socially stigmatized people help old ladies across the street and respectable citizens turn a blind eye to those who needed help.

How you look and what you do for work doesn't make you a good or bad person.

Your actions, or the lack of them, do. Those who seek the person in you will care only about your human side.

It is human to love, to believe, to fear, to wish, to help others and yourself. It's human to seek adventure, to find a spark in every situation life gives you, even if it is as small as a slice of bread and cheap salami. You can always make a smiley sandwich from it and enjoy the flavor with the gratitude of eating more than millions of others who are in greater need.

Not all of us will be billionaires; not all of us wish for that. The true measurement of courage is to accept our fate, to bring out the best in the present, and to work hard for the future we want to have. The courage to accept and to take action are two invaluable qualities.

Be curious and let your courage transform curiosity into adventure. After all, what is success if not a peaceful smile at the end of the day telling you that you did everything you could to transform your dreams into memories.

"It's folly to measure success in money or fame. Success is measured only by your ability to say yes to these two questions: Did I do the work I needed to do? Did I give it everything I had?"

--Cheryl Strayed

Be honest with yourself; trust your gut; and be charming, lively, and happy! Live your days as if they were your last!

What truly matters is to never cease learning. Stay a student, even if you think you've mastered a skill. Whatever tests you face in life, the lessons will be less painful if you face them with your best knowledge and an open mind to welcome any new information.

If you decide that there's nothing new under the sun for you to learn, that you know it all, most of the time life will prove you wrong. Those lessons are far harder to swallow because your overgrown ego won't let it go smoothly. It won't be as easy as it is for the girl in *Frozen* to sing *Let It Go*. You'll face one of the two great dangers mentioned in Chapter 3: You might be driven to prove yourself with the same weapon and to die again and again by it, or retreat to the grandstand and scream loudly that you're a champion.

You can learn something from every experience. There is not a single person who cannot teach you something. It doesn't matter the age, education, or profession. If you are open to new things, and you are willing to see and accept them, you'll never feel your time was wasted.

Just like the best opportunities, the most valuable experiences are not necessarily the loudest, the most active, or the most challenging ones. The most valuable ones are the ones that touch your heart. Strong emotions and feelings grant better and more memorable lessons than any soulless victories.

I bet you can remember what you were doing on 9/11. I bet you can still recall the time you made your mother cry for the first time. You can probably recall your first kiss and the time you went fishing with your dad and he told you what a great kid you were. Powerful emotions create memories that last.

That's why it is so important to put your heart into everything you do. Heartfelt memories stay with you. Courageous moments, which are heart-driven, stay with you, lift you, and make you a better person.

Be ready to fall, be hurt, cheated, made fun of, and still do what you do with all you have. Let others see who you are. Allow yourself to be the person you are. Have the courage to experience everything and fall, rise, live, and love.

Through the distance of this book, this is the best way I can express how many possibilities lay before you and how wonderful you are.

I really believe in you!

Yours truly,

Zoe

Endnotes

---

[i] Layton, Julia. How Fear Works? How Stuff Works. 2018.
https://science.howstuffworks.com/life/inside-the-mind/emotions/fear.htm

[ii] Gapminder. Extreme poverty trend. Gapminder. 2017.
https://www.gapminder.org/topics/extreme-poverty-trend/

[iii] Dave Ramsey. Financial Peace University. 2018.

[iv] Babsky, Evgeni. Boris Khodorov. Grigory Kositsky, Anatoly Zubkov, 'Conditioned-Reflex Activity of the Cerebral Cortex'. Human Physiology, in 2 vols. 2. Translated by Ludmila Aksenova; translation edited by H. C. Creighton (M.A., Oxon). Moscow: Mir Publishers. pp. 330–357. ISBN 5-03-000776-8. 1989.

www.ingramcontent.com/pod-product-compliance
Lightning Source LLC
Chambersburg PA
CBHW020107240426
43661CB00002B/57